THE COMPLETE GUIDE TO
KITTEN CARE

MARK EVANS
ANIMAL CARE

THE COMPLETE GUIDE TO
KITTEN CARE

To my Mum and Dad, and their cat Spring

Published in the United States by

Howell Book House
A Simon & Schuster Macmillan Company
1633 Broadway
New York, NY 10019

MACMILLAN is a registered trademark of Macmillan, Inc.

ISBN 0-87605-599-4

Library of Congress Cataloging-in-Publication Data available
upon request from the Library of Congress.

Manufactured in the People's Republic of China.

10 9 8 7 6 5 4 3 2 1

Contents

Introduction

Cats and people have shared each others' lives for centuries, and today pet cats are a very familiar part of our human society. In fact, in the UK they are even thought to outnumber pet dogs.

It is perhaps because cats are now such common household residents that there is a natural tendency for us to take their presence for granted. Cats are relatively easy to obtain, and there is an abundance of convenience products and services available to help us to look after them. It is all too easy to forget that – although they may share our homes and can have a significant impact on our lives – cats are wild at heart and are not born 'pre-programmed' to understand us or the way that we live.

To a greater or lesser extent, depending on their lifestyle, all cats have to adapt their natural instincts in order to live with people. And, just as they must learn about our human ways, so we should try to see life from their perspective. When we are interacting with cats, it is important to be able to interpret their body language to discover how they are feeling and what they are trying to say.

There is no doubt that the very best relationships between pet cats and people develop as a result of mutual understanding, tolerance and respect. A cat's trust must be earned, not expected. Ask any cat-owner and he or she will tell you that, if a person and a cat become great friends, it is because the cat – and not the person – has decided that it should be so.

Choosing a kitten

A successful friendship between you and your future cat will be built on solid foundations, laid well in advance. Time spent researching and planning before you obtain a kitten will pay dividends in the long term. The more effort you put into choosing your kitten and preparing yourself and your home for his arrival, the better able you will be to care for him properly, and the more likely you will be to become friends.

This may sound obvious, but it never ceases to surprise me how many people adopt a kitten purely on an impulse. It seems that young kittens have an extraordinary ability to make our hearts go to our heads and our brains sink to our boots!

Most people who adopt pedigree kittens choose those kittens purely because of the way they look, but this kind of approach can lead to problems. For instance, Siamese cats are the epitome of elegance,

but most individuals of this breed are extremely vocal animals, and this characteristic may become annoying to owners who like their peace and quiet. On a more practical note, Persian cats are undoubtedly glamorous but require considerable effort from their owners to keep their coats in top condition.

Equally likely to encounter problems are those people who adopt a cross-bred or a 'moggie' kitten simply by picking an individual who takes their fancy from the first litter on which they set their eyes: the ultimate marriage of convenience.

Early experiences

To make your decision in these ways is to overlook many important aspects of choosing the right kitten for you and your family. A kitten's early experiences in life will have a significant effect on the kind of cat that he becomes. For instance, a kitten who grows up in isolation from human contact – such as on a farm – is likely to be more 'wild' and independent than one brought up in a family home, and he may be unsuited to the lifestyle that you can give him. Before you select a kitten from a litter, you must consider all the options.

Our knowledge and understanding of cats – and our ability to look after them – will only improve through research, and this is an important part of my work as a veterinary surgeon.

My cat Gorbachov is lucky enough to be able to roam freely in safe surroundings. Like all cats, he has his own territory and is prepared to defend it from intruders if necessary.

Preparing for a new kitten

Getting ready for the arrival of your kitten will take time. You and all those who are to share his life will need to learn about the way cats live and behave, and about how to satisfy your kitten's unique mental and physical needs. You must decide whether you will give him access outdoors, and, if so, whether he will be free to roam or whether you will restrict his movements.

It will take you more than a few days to make your house and garden safe, to select and buy all the care products that you will need and to decide on what you are going to feed your kitten. But with these jobs organized in advance, you can then devote yourself to helping your kitten to settle into his new surroundings when he first comes to live with you.

Caring for a kitten

There is no single perfect way to care for a kitten. All cats have a great deal in common, but the individual whom you adopt will be quite unique. His precise care needs are therefore likely to differ from those of the cat next door, or from those of any other cat.

Being sensitive to your kitten's needs, and adapting the way that you look after him to meet them, is an art that you will learn through experience. You may turn to this book – or to any number of experts – whenever you wish for advice and guidance, but you are the only one who can make the final decisions relating

to your kitten's care. Like the rest of us you are bound to make some mistakes, but by using this book as a guide, keeping an open mind, adopting a flexible approach to the care of your kitten, accepting the limitations of your knowledge and being prepared to ask for help you will be able to remedy any mistakes quickly. More importantly, you will be much less likely to make those mistakes in the first place.

Using this book

This book is not intended to be a complete set of rules dictating how to look after a kitten, but is simply a guide to the most important issues that, in my view, all owners need to consider very carefully both before and after a feline companion comes into their lives. What I have written in the following pages is a mixture of the most up-to-date information I can find and my personal views based on years of experience of living with, looking after, treating and studying cats of all kinds.

As your kitten's owner, you must be prepared to take decisions on his behalf. The aim of this book is to make it easier for you to identify the decisions that you need to take, and to take them armed with knowledge rather than hearsay.

The book follows a logical progression through the history of the pet cat and the birth and early days of a litter of kittens, to the many preparations that you will need to make before going to choose your kitten (to avoid any confusion, I have referred to your kitten as 'he' throughout). Next, for the time when your kitten is actually living with you, comes detailed information on practical issues such as toileting, basic training and the lifestyle that you can give your kitten. A final section covers all aspects of preventive healthcare to keep him healthy as well as happy. Ideally, you should aim to read the book all the way through, and then refer back to specific sections as a general guide.

I have provided an overall philosophy on caring for a kitten, but only you can decide on the lifestyle that you will give to your own kitten. None of us is a perfect cat-owner and – as our cats cannot tell us what they think of the way that we look after them – none of us is ever likely to be. However, by relying on a mixture of scientific knowledge, experience and basic common sense, we should not go too far wrong.

What is a cat?

The cat has a fascinating history that can be traced back over thousands of years. In that time it has barely altered in shape and size, and has retained many of its wild instincts. However, cats are remarkably adaptable animals and will develop strong, loving relationships with those who treat them with kindness and respect.

The history of the pet cat

The bond that will develop between you and your kitten will be a new chapter in the story of man's remarkable relationship with the cat. It is an alliance that has spanned many centuries and taken many forms, with the cat adopting an assortment of roles including that of rat-catcher, religious totem, status symbol and companion. It is also a relationship that continues to evolve today, as pedigree breeds such as the Siamese and Abyssinian, and new breeds like the ragdoll and the sphynx become increasingly popular.

The big and small cats

There are about 25 different species in the cat family, but only one has been domesticated. It is not known why our domestic cat has made such a success of

living with us, while many other small cats – just as appealing to look at – are on the verge of extinction in their natural habitats.

The best-known of the big cats are the lion, the tiger, the leopard and the cheetah. These large, handsome animals can all be kept successfully in captivity, but none has been truly domesticated.

In terms of species, the big cats are significantly outnumbered by the small cats, but we know much less about them. Some small cats look bizarre, such as the otter-like jaguarundi of South America; or Pallas's cat, a shaggy, troll-like beast from the steppes of Asia. Most are beautifully marked, and many – such as the sand cat and the little spotted cat – share the domestic cat's appealing eyes and expression. Yet some of these cats are now endangered species, while the domestic cat numbers its population in hundreds of millions.

The African wild cat

The debate about the ancestor of our domestic cat has finally been settled by new technology similar to that of DNA 'fingerprinting'. The claims of the jungle cat, the leopard and the sand cat have been shown to be false. Domestic cats are in fact the true descendants of just one species: *Felis silvestris lybica*, the African wild cat.

The beautiful African wild cat is quite tolerant of humans, and in some areas of Africa still lives on the outskirts of villages, scavenging as well as hunting.

THE PROCESS OF DOMESTICATION

It is difficult to pinpoint exactly when domestication of the cat took place. The truth is probably that the cat domesticated itself, very gradually over several thousand years. For centuries its body did not change in shape at all, making it hard for archaeologists to decide whether bones from prehistoric settlements were those of wild cats killed for their fur, or of tame cats who had simply died of old age.

Some of the first European explorers of Africa found semi-tame wild cats tethered in foodstore huts to keep vermin at bay, and this may provide a clue as to how the cat came to be domesticated. It is also possible that wild cats became tamer not because humans wished it, but so that the cats could take advantage of easy prey such as rats and mice attracted by human foodstores.

Regardless of how it happened, once this working relationship between man and cat had been established the process of domestication could begin.

The cat in Ancient Egypt

The Ancient Egyptians were the first to depict the cat as a domestic animal. They are often given all the credit for domestication, but in fact they probably just added one chapter to the cat's relationship with man.

For much of the millennium before the birth of Christ, the cat was revered by the Egyptians as a sacred animal. The cat-headed fertility goddess Bast had a huge temple devoted to her at Bubastis, and the annual festival held in her honour attracted up to 750,000 worshippers. Thousands of cats were kept by priests in temples all over Egypt and, when the cats died, many were mummified and placed in tombs.

The similarities between many pet cats and their ancestors are striking, not only in terms of appearance but also in their stalking, hunting and territory-defending behaviour.

The Egyptian cats still looked very much like the African wild cats: their forelegs were long, and they sat with straight backs. For hundreds of years their coats were exclusively striped, or spotted like those of modern tabby cats. The first 'new' coat colour was pure black, which probably appeared as a mutation in one of the North African ports in about 500 BC.

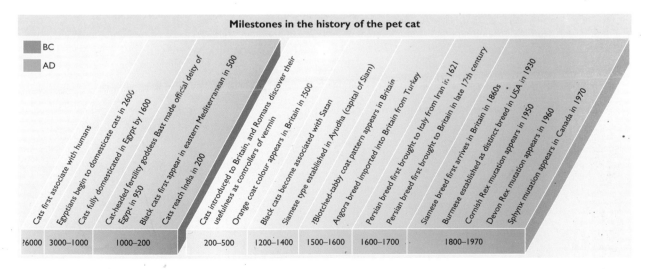

Milestones in the history of the pet cat

- BC
- AD

Cats first associate with humans
Egyptians begin to domesticate cats in 2600
Cats fully domesticated in Egypt by 1600
Cat-headed fertility goddess Bast made official deity of Egypt in 950
Black cats first appear in eastern Mediterranean in 500
Cats reach India in 200
Cats introduced to Britain, and Romans discover their usefulness as controllers of vermin
Orange coat colour appears in Britain in 1500
Black cats become associated with Satan
Siamese type established in Ayudha (capital of Siam)
Blotched-tabby coat pattern appears in Britain
Angora breed imported into Britain from Turkey
Persian breed first brought to Italy from Iran in 1621
Persian breed first brought to Britain in late 17th century
Siamese breed first arrives in Britain in 1860s
Burmese established as distinct breed in USA in 1930
Cornish Rex mutation appears in 1950
Devon Rex mutation appears in 1960
Sphynx mutation appears in Canada in 1970

| ?6000 | 3000–1000 | 1000–200 | 200–500 | 1200–1400 | 1500–1600 | 1600–1700 | 1800–1970 |

The next thousand years

The Egyptians guarded their cats jealously, but after the Roman defeat of the Egyptian empire in 30 BC domestic cats were free to spread to Europe. They appear to have been carried by traders, possibly as 'ships' cats'. The first cats to arrive in Britain, in about AD 200, had probably hitched a ride along the trade route running from the Mediterranean, up the Rhône, down the Rhine and across the English Channel.

The Romans kept cats primarily as pets, as well as to control vermin, but the Celts seem to have regarded them as having a mystic significance, as the remains of cats sacrificed to local deities have been found.

During the Dark Ages, cats were prized much more for their value as pest-controllers, although some cats must undoubtedly have been kept as pets.

The 13th to 16th centuries

This was not a good time to be a cat – at least, not in Europe. By the early Middle Ages, Christianity had absorbed many elements of other religions, including cat-worship traceable back to the original Egyptian cult of Bast. However, from the 13th century onwards these cults were purged, cat-keeping was frowned upon and many thousands of cats were put to death.

Cats were thought to have supernatural powers, and became symbols of the Devil himself. Their ability to fall from great heights without injury was ascribed to demonic intervention, and their 'eye-shine' was thought to be caused by an unholy alliance with the moon. It is a tribute to the cat's resilience that it was able to survive these centuries of persecution.

The 17th to 19th centuries

Religious persecution waned in the 17th century, but the Puritans frowned upon pet-keeping and it was not until the mid-18th century that the idea of keeping cats became acceptable. Even then, many cats must have led short and unhappy lives, as concern for animal welfare was uncommon until the mid-19th century.

The 20th century

Cats have increased in favour throughout this century. Their cleanliness, independent natures and generally placid temperaments make them well-suited to urban living, and it is easy to forget that their popularity is a relatively recent development.

This typical short-haired, cross-bred pet cat is smaller and has shorter legs than his wild ancestor. However, he is still an agile, athletic animal, well-suited to acting as a formidable predator when the need arises.

ear flap — withers — abdomen — flank — tail — hip — upper jaw — lower jaw — neck — shoulder — elbow — forearm — wrist — chest wall (rib cage) — forefoot (with five clawed toes) — hind foot (with four clawed toes) — point of hock (heel)

THE MODERN BREEDS

Today, few domestic cats have the long-legged, lithe body plan of the Ancient Egyptian cats. It is very likely that, as these Egyptian cats spread both northwards into Europe and eastwards into Asia, they interbred with local wild-cat populations. This process can certainly explain the development of the short-legged and comparatively stocky cats typical of Europe, as well as the fine-boned oriental breeds, which appear to be cousins of the European wild cat and the Indian desert cat respectively.

Changes in coat colour

After black, the orange coat colour of cats is probably the oldest mutation. Other simple mutations have created the white-paws-and-chin pattern, the various types of long hair, and the dilution effect that turns black to 'blue' and orange to cream. The colourpoints of the Siamese, which occur on the coolest areas of the body due to temperature differences at the skin surface (see page 109), are also an ancient mutation, as is the stumpy tail of the Japanese bobtail cat.

The 'typical' cat is often taken to be a blotched tabby, but this coat pattern is actually only 300 years old, and originated in England (possibly in London). Today, this type of coat is most common in Britain, the Netherlands and in places settled by British colonists such as Canada, Australia and New Zealand.

Changes in appearance

The creation of breeds based on specific combinations of coat colour and body shape is a phenomenon that dates back little further than the first cat show, held in Britain in 1871. For example, the temple cats of Thailand are 'oriental' in appearance, but not all have the colourpoints of the pedigree Siamese, or its wedge-shaped head. Many breeds are even more recent: the Burmese, for instance, dates back only to the 1930s.

In comparison with the development of dog breeds, there is little scope for producing variation in the cat without creating extreme deviations in anatomy. As a result, the newest cat breeds tend to be deformed oddities such as the very short-legged munchkin and the hairless sphynx. Many people – myself included – would argue that developing such breeds will have a detrimental effect on cat welfare. At present, however, almost all pet cats have bodies similar to those of their wild ancestors, and long may they remain that way.

The cat's body is an extremely complex biological machine, whose individual parts work efficiently together. Whatever their outward appearance, all cats contain the same basic internal components.

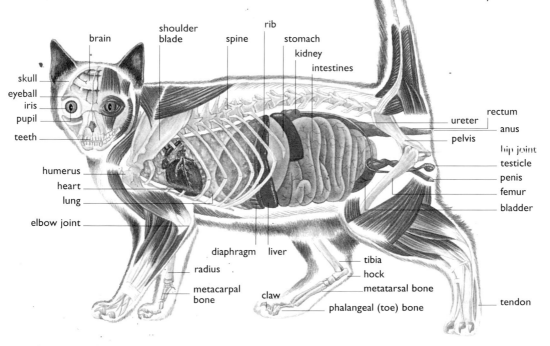

brain shoulder blade spine rib stomach kidney intestines

skull
eyeball
iris
pupil
teeth

humerus
heart
lung

elbow joint

radius
metacarpal bone

diaphragm liver claw

phalangeal (toe) bone

tibia
hock
metatarsal bone

rectum
ureter
anus
pelvis
hip joint
testicle
penis
femur
bladder

tendon

Your kitten's life starts here

The early days of a kitten's life – both before birth and after it – are very exciting. If you plan to invite a kitten into your life in the future, or if he is already with you but you would like to have been there when his life began, this part of my book is for you.

The mere concept of life before birth – of one living animal growing and developing inside another until it is ready to be born – fills most of us with wonder. If you have had a baby, or if you know someone who has done so, this is a subject that you have probably discussed many times. With humans, it all starts with a kiss; with cats, it's not so different.

THE MATING GAME

Adult male (tom) cats are usually sexually active and interested in mating at any time of the year, although some scientists believe that they produce the most sperm during the spring and summer months.

However, adult females (queens) are only sexually active within a specific breeding season each year. The precise timing of the breeding season for a particular queen will depend on daylight length: in the UK, for example, the breeding season for most cats extends from January through to September, but some queens kept in conditions of artificial lighting may be able to breed all year round.

Before intercourse takes place, the queen is literally pinned to the ground by her mate.

The queen in heat

During the breeding season, a mature queen has clear periods of sexual activity called heats, during which she will mate (see page 123). Most matings between pure-bred cats are orchestrated by responsible owners and usually take place at the toms' homes. Of course, some matings – particularly those between cross-bred cats or moggies (see page 44) – are far less formal events arranged by the cats themselves.

'Calling'

When a queen comes into heat, she begins a pattern of specific behaviour known as 'calling'. At first, she may be especially affectionate towards her owner and engage in more head- and flank-rubbing than normal. She will roll on the ground and become very vocal.

At the peak of her heat, the queen will adopt a characteristic posture in front of her owner or another cat. She will lie with her forelegs stretched out flat on the ground, with her head lying between them. Her rear end will be raised, and she will stand on tiptoes with her hindlegs bent. With her tail curled round to one side to expose her genitals, she will tread up and down with her hind feet.

The queen will continue to vocalize and to adopt this behaviour pattern for five to 10 days in the hope of attracting one or more toms to mate with her. Her invitation is both noisy and visually obvious, and one that few – if any – normal toms will ignore.

The sexual act

When a tom finds the queen, or she is introduced to one at a stud, he may make chirping calls before copulating with her. The mating is usually a shortlived affair. The tom will seize the queen by her scruff with his mouth and will then climb over her, using his forepaws to grip the front of her body. The queen will respond by dropping her front end nearer to the ground and raising her rear end.

The mating position of the tom and queen

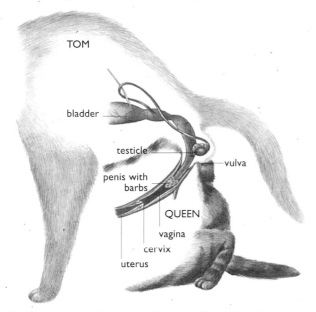

Having ejaculated his sperm the tom will quickly dismount. As he withdraws his penis, its barbs stimulate the queen's vaginal wall in a process thought to help induce ovulation.

Stepping from side to side using his hindlegs, with his whole body swaying, the tom then arches his back and penetrates the queen. A few very energetic pelvic thrusts for between five and 15 seconds precede the ejaculation of his sperm.

After ejaculating, the tom dismounts and quickly disappears, as the queen normally cries out and may try to strike him. She has good reason for her reaction. On the tom's penis are backward-pointing barbs which stimulate the queen's vulva during intercourse and the withdrawal, so helping to induce ovulation (see above, right). For this reason, mating – and particularly the removal of the tom's penis – must be painful for her.

Post-coital behaviour

As soon as the tom has withdrawn, the queen rolls frantically on the ground. Experts believe that this may encourage the sperm to flow from the queen's vagina through her cervix and into her uterus.

During this time, both the queen and the tom will lick their own genitals clean in preparation for another mating: in fact, there may be several matings between them over the next hour or so. Given the opportunity, a queen may mate with a number of males over the following four or five days of the same heat.

Ovulation

Ovulation occurs 23 to 30 hours after mating and, on average, non-pedigree queens will ovulate four eggs. Of course, there is no guarantee that all the fertilized eggs will develop into kittens, and more than four eggs may be ovulated. Most non-pedigree cats actually give birth to between three and seven kittens.

Oriental breeds tend to have larger litter sizes – sometimes of more than 10 kittens – while pedigree long-haired breeds often have small litters of just two or three kittens. It is unusual for a queen of any type or breed to give birth to a single kitten.

Conception

Once an egg is fertilized by a sperm, a reaction occurs that prevents another sperm from entering the same egg. However, in theory, a queen who produces a litter of kittens having mated with a number of different toms may have had each one of her eggs fertilized by sperm from a different father.

FERTILIZATION

Although only a single sperm should be required to fertilize an egg, scientists estimate that perhaps one million sperm are actually needed to create a suitable environment for fertilization to occur. An unknown number of the queen's eggs may be successfully fertilized within the tubes that lead from the ovaries to the uterus, and it will then be about another week before the fertilized eggs reach the uterus itself.

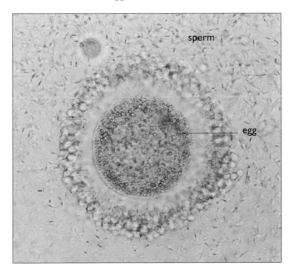

LIFE BEFORE BIRTH

Kittens are largely helpless at birth, and have to rely almost entirely on their mother for the first three to four weeks of their lives. This is because they spend a comparatively short time – just nine weeks on average – in their mother's uterus.

During those nine weeks, the developing kittens enjoy a stress-free existence. Completely enclosed in individual life-support systems in the darkness of the queen's uterus, they are kept nourished, warm and protected.

The journey to the uterus

For the first two weeks after conception has occurred, the kitten-to-be, or embryo, is barely larger than a pin-head. First it travels down the tube from the ovary to the uterus. On its journey, the single cell from which the whole kitten will form divides into two, then four, then eight cells and so on, until it becomes a solid but microscopic ball of cells.

All the developing embryos – each one destined to become a kitten in the same litter – reach the uterus between 13 and 17 days after the eggs were ovulated. Once they arrive there, the embryos tend to spread out evenly throughout the two sides, or horns, of the uterus and then embed themselves securely in its wall (see above, right).

A cut-away view of the queen's uterus

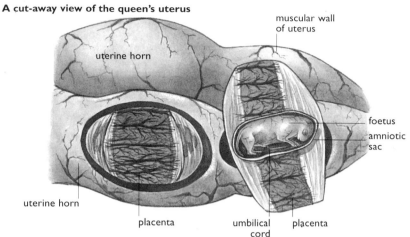

The foetuses are spread along the 'arms' of the Y-shaped uterus; each is enclosed in its own life-support system.

The developing embryos

As the embryos develop further, some cells begin to create the kittens' bodies. Others form the membranes that surround them, as well as the placentas that will connect their blood systems to that of their mother.

By about 16 days after conception, the embryos' heads and backbones will have started to develop.

Unlike a pregnant bitch, who starts to put on weight from week five of pregnancy, a pregnant queen puts on weight consistently. Initially, most of this extra weight is body fat.

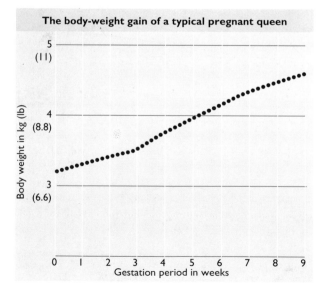

The body-weight gain of a typical pregnant queen

Body weight in kg (lb)

5 (11)
4 (8.8)
3 (6.6)

Gestation period in weeks
0 1 2 3 4 5 6 7 8 9

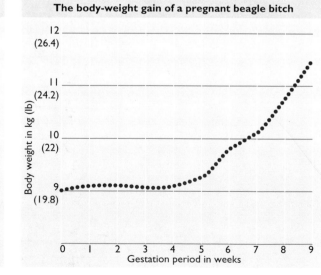

The body-weight gain of a pregnant beagle bitch

Body weight in kg (lb)

12 (26.4)
11 (24.2)
10 (22)
9 (19.8)

Gestation period in weeks
0 1 2 3 4 5 6 7 8 9

The embryos' placentas are not functional until about day 22, so for the time being they obtain their nourishment from a built-in food source called the yolk sac. By the time the yolk is depleted, each embryo is floating in its own sac of fluid, and is connected to its life-giving placenta by a rope of blood vessels called the umbilical cord.

The limbs, head and eyes then begin to develop rapidly, and after four weeks all the kittens' organs have formed, although they are not fully developed. At this stage the embryos are just 25–30 mm (1 in) long, curled up in the foetal position (see opposite).

The foetal stage

From four weeks after conception to birth at about nine weeks, the kittens are referred to as foetuses. During this time their organs mature and they grow quickly, doubling in length once between 28 days and 40 days, and again by eight weeks.

Touch • This is the first sense to develop, and appears from about 28 days onwards. What use the foetuses may make of the ability to feel their surroundings is unknown, although it is thought that it may help to control the action of the limbs. This movement can be detected from the seventh week of pregnancy onwards.

Taste • This sense probably also begins to function before birth, enabling the kittens to taste the amniotic fluid in which they are floating. It is possible that they may even be able to learn a little about some of the foods that their mother is eating at this very early stage of their lives, as certain flavours can survive digestion and reach the amniotic fluid.

Balance • This is the next sense to develop in the foetuses. It begins to function at about eight weeks after conception has occurred.

Hearing and sight • These senses develop later on; newly born kittens are both deaf and blind.

This queen is eight weeks into her pregnancy, and will soon give birth. To nourish the developing foetuses inside her, she is likely by this stage to be eating approximately 25 per cent more food than before she conceived.

PREGNANCY STATISTICS

• The average length of pregnancy in the cat is between 63 and 65 days, but there are reports of pregnancies being as short as 59 days, and as long as 70 days.

• At birth, a kitten is about 12.5 cm (5 in) in length, although the exact size will vary between breeds. If a queen is carrying a large litter, each kitten may also be slightly smaller than the average for that breed.

THE PREGNANT QUEEN

The first external sign that a queen has conceived comes after about three weeks. Her nipples – until then quite small and pale – enlarge and become bright pink in colour; the hair that surrounds the nipples also recedes slightly. By day 40 the queen's breasts should be obviously enlarged. However, her behaviour will barely change until about two weeks before giving birth (in the wild, a pregnant queen spends more time hunting than usual to satisfy her increased need for nutrients during the later stages of pregnancy and lactation). Unlike the female dog, whose greatest increase in weight occurs in the final three weeks of pregnancy, a queen will gain weight fairly steadily (see page 14). Her total weight gain will depend on the number of kittens that she is carrying, but she may put on as much as 1.5 kg (3 lb 5 oz) in weight. Her abdomen will be noticeably swollen, and she may move awkwardly during late pregnancy if she is expecting a large litter.

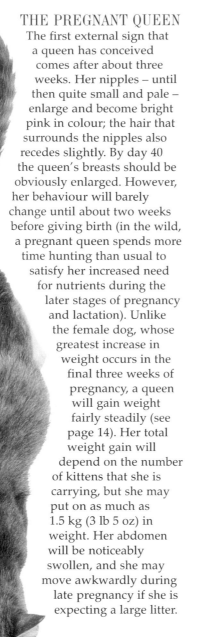

Viewed from above, a queen who is due to go into labour has a very obviously distended abdomen. At this stage, it can be difficult to palpate the individual foetuses through the abdominal wall.

Ultrasound examination of a queen is carried out with a piece of equipment similar to that used to investigate pregnancy in a woman. The procedure is quite painless, and most queens will submit to it without too much fuss.

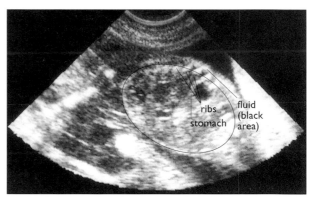

The image created by an ultrasound machine is called a scan, and can be used to confirm pregnancy as early as the second week. The ringed area on this picture shows a cross-section through the abdomen of a foetus on day 28 of pregnancy.

Confirming pregnancy

There are a number of techniques that a vet can use to confirm pregnancy in a queen.

Ultrasound examination • This involves the use of a machine very similar to that used to confirm pregnancy in women (see above). In experienced hands, an ultrasound examination may be used to detect the presence of individual embryos in the uterus just 14 days after mating has occurred.

Abdominal palpation • By gently feeling through the body wall, it is possible in some queens to feel the growing foetuses inside the uterus. This is easiest between days 16 and 26 (as pregnancy develops

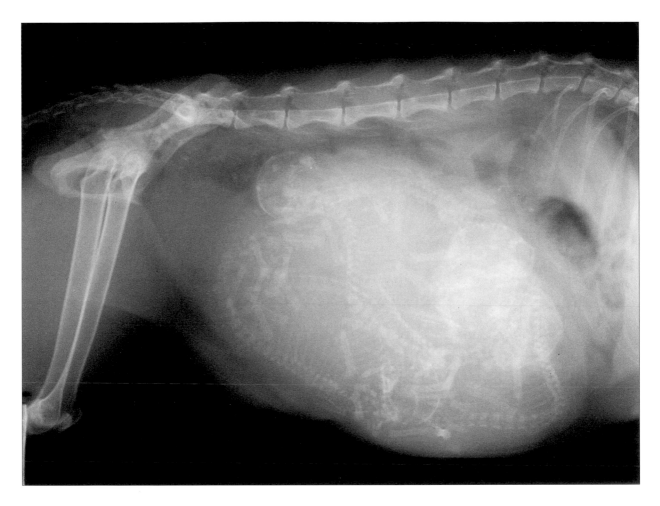

This X-ray picture was taken with the pregnant queen lying on her side. The many faint white lines in the middle of the abdominal area are the tiny bones of the foetal skeletons.

beyond this stage, it can actually become more difficult to distinguish individual foetuses).

Taking an X-ray picture • After day 40 of pregnancy, an X-ray picture of the queen's abdomen should reveal the tiny foetal skeletons (see above).

Listening for foetal heartbeats • This can be done using a stethoscope in late pregnancy. The foetal heart-rate is faster than that of the mother.

Pre-birth behaviour

In the week before the birth the queen will be less active than normal, but she will usually spend a considerable amount of time searching for a suitable place to have her kittens. She may be persuaded to adopt a site chosen by her owner, but some queens become especially nervous at this stage.

In adopting this behaviour, the queen is driven by an instinctive desire to find a secret place in which her kittens will be both safe and sheltered. This is because, in the wild, newborn kittens will be preyed upon by birds, dogs and other predators. The queen's instinct is therefore telling her to search out an inaccessible nook or cranny as a nest-site.

The old custom of drowning unwanted kittens at birth as a method of controlling cat numbers may also have played a part in perpetuating this secretive behaviour, because female kittens born to those queens who instinctively gave birth out of the reach of people were more likely to survive to give birth themselves.

More confident queens may choose familiar but open locations in which to give birth to their kittens, such as their owners' beds!

Birth

Nine weeks – give or take a few days – after their parents mated, it is time for the still-helpless foetuses to prepare to face the outside world. Now fully developed, they take a central part in initiating a remarkable chain of events that results in their physical and forceful eviction from the security of their mother's body. Labour, or kittening, has begun, and the kittens are about to be born.

Thanks to ante-natal classes, most people have a good idea of what to expect during the birth of a baby, but for first-time queens there is no such information. We must assume that, although they feel very strange and have an unusual stomach-ache, they have no idea what will happen next. They simply get on with the birth, guided by their natural instincts.

THE ONSET OF LABOUR

During the first stage of labour, the queen's body prepares for action in a number of ways.

Getting ready

The contractions of the uterus at the start of labour may make the queen feel uncomfortable. Her pulse quickens, and she begins to breathe more rapidly.

A pregnant queen will spend time searching for a suitable nest-site in which she feels confident to go into labour and bring her kittens into the world.

Her body temperature drops by a degree or so: this may happen just 12 hours before giving birth, but in some cases occurs up to a day or so in advance of the kittening. Close to the time of labour, milk may begin to appear at the queen's nipples.

Just before giving birth, the queen will retreat to her nest and will clean herself thoroughly. The smell of her saliva may act as a cue to help her newborn kittens find her nipples in order to feed.

The birth canal

For the kittens to be born, the queen's birth canal must change to allow their safe passage.

Her pelvis and its ligaments begin to relax, and her vagina, vulva and the other tissues surrounding them soften so that they can stretch without tearing as each kitten is forced through the opening.

Closed during pregnancy to seal off the uterus, the queen's muscular cervix also undergoes complex changes that will allow it to open fully when the time is right for the first kitten to be born. Her uterus starts to contract, and the placentas – having supplied each foetus with life-giving blood during pregnancy – begin to 'unplug' themselves from its wall.

Preparing for birth

The foetuses themselves must also prepare to become kittens capable of surviving outside their mother's body. Two of their most serious problems will be breathing and coping with the cold. Of course, living underwater inside their mother's uterus, there is no way in which they can test their lungs before birth. However, alterations in the levels of certain hormones in their bodies are thought to help to cause the necessary changes in their lungs that will allow them to start working for the first time on demand. In addition, to prepare for a colder environment than that of the uterus, each foetus rapidly builds special energy stores that can be burned off after birth to help in the production of body heat.

In order to avoid becoming stuck during the birth process, each foetus adopts a streamlined pose ready to 'dive' or 'jump' backwards through the birth canal if necessary. During pregnancy, all the foetuses normally lie curled up with their legs and their heads tucked in, but now they become more active and will soon uncurl their bodies, straighten out their legs and roll over. This stage of labour may last between two and 12 hours, during which the queen may be very restless and may vocalize frequently.

THE FIRST KITTEN

The strong contractions of the uterus eventually push the first foetus through the cervix and into the queen's pelvis, and, as soon as she feels it there, the queen will begin to strain. By contracting her abdominal muscles at the correct time, she helps to push the foetus on through her birth canal.

The 'water bag'

The first thing to appear at the queen's vulva is likely to be a 'water bag' – one of two fluid-filled sacs that surround each foetus during pregnancy. The bag may break in the birth canal but, if not, it will either rupture due to the pressure of straining, or will be broken by the queen chewing at it. We must assume that, to her, the bag is a strange object that should be removed: she presumably has no idea of what is in it.

With each contraction and each strain, the kitten moves on through the birth canal, his passage made easier by the lubricating effect of the sac membranes that still surround his body.

Most kittens are born head-first, but as many as four out of 10 will enter the world backwards. The delivery is eased by the slippery membranes that surround each kitten.

A cut-away view of the queen's birth canal

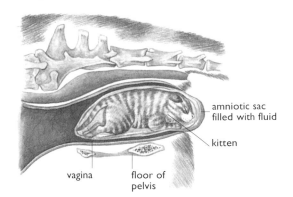

amniotic sac filled with fluid

kitten

vagina

floor of pelvis

The presence of a kitten in the part of the birth canal within the queen's pelvis stimulates her to strain, which she does using her abdominal muscles.

The delivery

The kitten's head is relatively large compared to the rest of his body, and the queen has to push hard to squeeze it through her birth canal. Once the head is through, however, the rest of the kitten's body usually follows fairly quickly. The queen may call out loudly as the kitten is born.

From the onset of straining, it will generally take a queen between five and 60 minutes to deliver her first kitten. This interval is normally the longest in queens who are giving birth to their first litters.

The queen instinctively rasps away the membranes from her kitten immediately after the birth, and will also bite through the umbilical cord if it has not already broken.

Immediate aftercare

Most queens are instinctively gifted mothers, and undertake the care of their kittens quite naturally. If a queen lives with other female cats, she may also receive their assistance in caring for her kittens, just as some queens do in the wild (see page 37).

The queen's first priority is to get her new kitten breathing as quickly as possible. To prevent him from suffocating, she nibbles away at the sac membranes that still surround him, and rasps them from the kitten's face using her rough tongue.

She does not stop there: by continuing to lick and nuzzle her kitten in order to clean him, she stimulates him to breathe. The queen is driven to clean her kitten in this way by the smell and taste of the amniotic fluid in which he is still covered. A kitten's first breath is generally more of a gasp than a breath as he attempts to inflate his lungs for the very first time.

POOR MOTHERS

Occasionally a queen may reject one or more of her kittens, and may fail to remove the sac membranes from his face or stimulate him to breathe. She may even eat the kitten. This kind of abnormal mothering behaviour is more common in inexperienced mothers, but some queens never become competent midwives.

The queen's next task is to dry her kitten: left wet, he will rapidly chill and may die. So she continues to lick him, and moves him towards her breasts for food and warmth. If necessary, she also breaks his umbilical cord by chewing through it with her teeth.

A newborn kitten's first priority is to find his way to a nipple in order to feed. Close to his mother, he will also share her body heat, without which he would be unlikely to survive.

BROTHERS AND SISTERS

With the first frantic moments over, the queen will start to clean herself up, but she may not have much of a rest. The second kitten – if there is one – could be born within five minutes, although he may arrive up to one hour later. He will receive the same meticulous attention from his mother as the first kitten.

Any further kittens in the litter will normally be delivered at five- to 60-minute intervals, but there may be pauses in labour of up to several hours. In between kittens the queen may be very restless, and she may pace around her nest.

During the delivery of the kittens there will probably be a dark-brown discharge from the queen's vulva, which is caused by the breakdown of the placentas.

How long does labour take?

Every kittening is different, so there is no set pattern. In most cases it is all over within six hours, but, if there have been any long pauses during the labour, it can take up to 24 hours. As each kitten has his own life-support placenta, such lengthy labours do not normally cause problems, provided that the pauses are not due to a kitten becoming stuck in the birth canal.

After giving birth, the queen may be aggressive to any animal that she believes may threaten her kittens.

After the kittening, a queen has many new responsibilities. She must protect, feed and clean up after her kittens, and will do so even though she may be exhausted herself.

FIRST MILK

Having been cleaned up and dried off thoroughly, each of the kittens searches for a nipple and begins taking the most important meal of his life: colostrum.

This first milk contains very special substances called antibodies which, if consumed within 24 hours of birth, will provide the new kittens with temporary protection against the diseases to which their mother is immune. These will include any infections against which she has been vaccinated or from which she has suffered herself in the past (see pages 118–21).

Good food

After the birth of each kitten, parts of their placentas will remain inside the queen's body. Called afterbirths, these are pushed out by the queen either within a few minutes of delivering the kittens or later on during the labour. They should all be delivered within two hours of the last kitten being born.

As soon as the afterbirths appear, the queen's first reaction is to eat them. This is an instinctive behaviour: in the wild, afterbirths are an important and nutritious form of food in the days after giving birth when the queen is unable to hunt.

Early life

The life of a cat is generally divided up into four phases: neonatal, socialization, juvenile and adult (see page 23). It may surprise you to discover that not just the first, but also the second of these stages is likely to be over before you bring your new kitten home at about eight weeks of age (see page 36).

The milestones that a kitten will pass in his early development remain something of a mystery to many new owners, but knowledge of them can enhance the pleasure of getting to know a new feline companion.

Understanding kittens

There is also a more serious reason for understanding a kitten's very early development. Many aspects of his character will be forged during the first eight weeks of life, and several types of long-lasting behavioural problems can stem from inappropriate surroundings at this early stage. Armed with this knowledge, you will know what to look out for when choosing a kitten, as well as what questions to ask of the people who have been caring for him from his birth.

Wild instincts

Never forget that kittens are not instinctively friendly towards people. Even after thousands of years of being involved with man, the cat is not a fully domesticated species. For instance, in some parts of the world – such as the Australian outback and some oceanic islands – cats live, breed and roam without human contact of any kind. As a result, these cats are as wary of people as any other wild animal would be.

It is only because kittens can learn to trust people at an early age that we are able to keep cats as pets at all. They inherit the potential to become pets from their mothers and fathers, but this potential still needs considerable input from their human companions if it is to be fully realized.

By far the most effective time for this to happen is during the first weeks of a kitten's life, and this is why it is so important for all owners to understand both the mental and physical development that a kitten undergoes during this period.

When very young, the kittens in a litter are nannied and nurtured by their mother, and they will learn from her what it is to be a cat and how to behave as one. However, regular human contact is also important from an early age.

Even at the age of just four weeks (above), kittens are gaining increased independence from their mother and are starting to explore on their own.

In spite of their new-found independence (right), at four weeks the kittens have not yet been weaned on to solid food, and still depend on the queen for milk as well as for warmth and comfort. The queen will continue to watch over her kittens diligently, and will bring them back to the nest when they venture too far afield.

Phases of development

In comparison with young puppies, kittens mature fairly quickly. Compared with children, of course, both kittens and puppies develop extremely rapidly.

A kitten's development to adulthood is divided into the following phases.

Neonatal phase • In the first two weeks of his life, a kitten is almost entirely helpless and relies on his mother to fulfil his needs.

Socialization phase • This phase starts in the third or fourth week of life, and is the period when a kitten is most receptive to features of his environment, including people and other animals (see page 31). It begins about a week earlier than in the puppy (for whom a separate, so-called 'transition' phase is recognized before the socialization phase), and ends about four weeks earlier than in the puppy.

Juvenile phase • This phase starts at eight to nine weeks. It is the least understood of all the stages of a cat's life, which is perhaps unfortunate given that it is the time when the cat's relationship with his new owner is established.

Adult phase • A kitten will normally reach sexual maturity at the age of about seven months, but will not attain his adult body weight for another five months or so. Physically, a cat's body at one year old is considered to be in a similar condition to that of a 16-year-old child; by two years old he is more like a 21-year-old person. Each successive year for a cat is roughly equivalent to four human years.

Week one

As soon as the whole litter has been delivered, the queen will encircle her kittens with her body, and will then stay beside them for virtually every minute of the first 24 hours. Even after cleaning them up thoroughly, she will continue to lick and nuzzle them, stimulating them to feed. Her first milk, colostrum (see page 21), is different in composition from the milk that she will produce from about the third day onwards.

On average, kittens at birth weigh just 100 g (4 oz). Kittens with birth weights of less than 80 g (3 oz) are unlikely to thrive. Although almost entirely helpless, newborn kittens are still more advanced than some other young mammals. For example, they are already furry, whereas rats and mice are born naked.

Food and sleep

For the first few days the kittens alternate between feeding and sleeping, and do little else. They 'twitch' frequently in their sleep, possibly because they are dreaming. So-called 'quiet' sleep, which alternates with dreaming sleep in the adult cat, will appear gradually during the next few weeks.

A queen will devote herself entirely to her kittens' care for the first 24 hours. As she suckles them and protects them while they sleep, internally her body begins to return to normal.

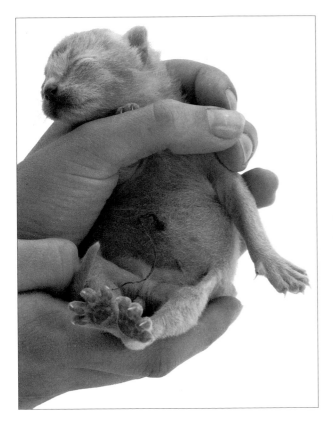

In their first week of life kittens are very fragile creatures, but they must be handled in order to check that they are healthy. The remnant of the umbilical cord will quickly shrivel and drop off, leaving a tiny scar.

Keeping warm

At birth, kittens are incapable of maintaining their own body temperatures, and this is one reason why it is so important for the first few days that they lie in contact with their mother's warm belly.

When the queen leaves the kittens very briefly, they will attempt to drag themselves into a so-called 'sleep heap'. Huddling together in a pile like this enables them to conserve their body heat more effectively.

Simple movements

In the first week, the kittens are able to move about to a limited degree by 'rowing' themselves along with their forelegs (these develop faster than the hindlegs). This method of locomotion is sufficient to enable the kittens to reach their mother's abdomen if they have been accidentally pushed away – perhaps during a particularly vigorous bout of washing.

DEVELOPING SENSES

Newborn kittens have a fairly limited appreciation of the world into which they have been delivered. Their eyelids are firmly closed, and their ears are blocked by ridges of skin. However, their senses of touch and smell are already fairly well-developed, and for the moment these are all that they need to ensure that they can find their mother and feed from her.

By the fifth day of life, the kittens' ears are starting to function properly, and they will begin to make very basic responses to noises if they are sufficiently loud.

The rooting reflex

The kittens locate their mother by her warmth and her smell. Once in contact with her, a kitten will crawl up and along the queen's belly, turning his head from side to side in search of a nipple.

When a nipple has been located, the feel of it on the kitten's snout initiates a wonderful piece of behaviour called the rooting reflex, in which the kitten pulls his head back and then lunges forward with his mouth open. If this results in the successful attachment to a nipple, the powerful sucking reflex takes over.

Day two onwards

Despite their limited abilities, kittens begin to learn about their environment from day two. Sucking is purely instinctive at first, but now becomes associated with the smell of the queen. The kittens also learn the smell of the nest, which they can sniff to find their way home if they are pushed away or fall out of the nest.

If a kitten is isolated, cold or hurt, he will emit a surprisingly loud distress call that elicits an instant response from the queen. In fact, new mothers seem more aware of what their newborn kittens sound like than what they look like. Unwittingly, they may even attempt to lie on top of their kittens until they are warned off by a sudden burst of squeaking.

By the end of the week a kitten can crawl for a distance of up to 50 cm (20 in). He will also attempt to support his weight if his body is gently supported by a person's hand.

A one-week-old kitten's body length is 15 cm (6 in).

Week two

The kittens are now growing rapidly, and they are developing new abilities almost daily, but the queen is still very much in charge during the second week of their lives. Although she will be beginning to spend a little more time away from them, she still initiates their frequent bouts of feeding by lying down beside her kittens, and nuzzling and licking them.

Feeding behaviour

By this stage, the kittens have come to realize that it is the nipples towards the back of their mother's belly that produce the most milk. The stronger and more active members of the litter will therefore attempt to monopolize these nipples.

While they are sucking, the kittens use their front paws to 'knead' on either side of the teats to stimulate the flow of milk. They will often purr loudly while feeding. If all the kittens do this at the same time, and the mother joins in as well, the resulting chorus of contentment can be heard from some distance!

A kitten who has become separated from the rest of the litter will call to attract the attention of his mother. She will then pick him up in her mouth, and carry him back to the nest.

NEST HYGIENE

Until their fourth week, kittens are unable to urinate or defecate voluntarily, and the queen is completely responsible for their hygiene and for that of the nest. She stimulates the kittens to eliminate their wastes by grooming them vigorously under their tails, and then promptly swallows everything that they produce.

In this way, the queen can keep the nest clean and hygienic until the kittens are old enough to leave it to use a litter-tray (see pages 30–1).

Learning to crawl

Although the muscles that control their limbs are already maturing fast, in the second week the kittens still propel themselves about by crawling.

The scruff reflex

Occasionally one kitten will still be sucking when his mother stands up to leave the nest, and will hang on for long enough to be dragged a short distance from it. By this stage he will have learned the smell of the nest and can use this to orientate himself as he crawls back towards it, but if the kitten is more than a very short distance from his litter mates he will probably begin to emit his distress call (see page 25).

The queen should then return to retrieve the kitten, which she will do by holding on to him by the loose skin on the back of his neck and picking him up in her mouth. Beneath this area of the kitten's skin are nerve-endings that trigger a special behaviour called the scruff reflex, which causes the kitten's body to go limp and his tail and legs to curl up out of harm's way. This makes his body much easier for the queen to carry.

Sensory development

Sight • The kittens' vision matures rapidly during the second week, provided that their eyes are open (this may happen at any time from the middle of the first week to the middle of the third week). Female kittens' eyes tend to open before those of males, and there is also a genetic influence:

kittens whose eyes open in the first week tend to have parents whose eyes also opened early. The first sign is that the eyelids begin to peel apart to reveal the eyes, which are always blue at this stage. The optic fluid that lies between the lens and the retina is cloudy at first (this normally clears during the sixth week), and the pupils do not start to contract in bright light for at least 24 hours after the opening of the eyes. As a result, a kitten's eyesight is probably fairly poor initially.

Hearing • During the second week, the kittens' ear flaps begin to unfold and stand upright. At the same time, the ear canals that connect the flaps to the ear drums open out, allowing the kittens to hear much more clearly than they were able to do by the end of the first week. They will now show an obvious reaction to a range of different sounds – especially to those made by other cats – by lifting and turning their heads, sniffing and swivelling their ears from side to side.

The kittens' world will start to seem a very different place as their hearing improves. Their eyes also begin to open at this stage, enabling them to see a little for the first time.

Increased abilities

By the end of their second week, the kittens will have become a great deal more lively than before. They may try to stand, as their forelegs will now be reasonably well co-ordinated and their hindlegs strong enough to support their weight. They should also be able to extend their claws: these are still quite soft, but may come in useful when the kittens are trying to keep their balance during their first tottering steps.

A two-week-old kitten's body length is 17.5 cm (7 in).

Week three

The kittens' perception of the world changes rapidly in week three as their hearing and eyesight continue to develop further. They soon learn how to locate the approximate direction from which a sound is coming, and a few days later are able to follow the direction of a sound that is moving – perhaps that of their mother giving her chirruping 'kitten call' to reassure the litter as she returns to the nest.

Improved vision

A few days later, the kittens can track a moving object by sight alone. By the end of this third week they will have a good mental picture of their surroundings, and will use sight rather than smell to find their way back to the nest. However, the kittens still cannot judge the actual distance of objects: to do this requires so-called binocular vision, and the parts of their brains that co-ordinate this have yet to mature.

Physical development

The rooting reflex, which helped the kittens to locate the queen's nipples when they were still blind (see page 25), now disappears.

Although the kittens still sleep for 60–70 per cent of the time, they are very active when they are awake. By this stage, they should have complete control over their hindlegs as well as over their forelegs, although the two sets of nervous reflexes that control walking in each pair of legs are not properly co-ordinated with each other. As a result, the kittens will sometimes tend to look as though their back ends are attempting to walk in a different direction to that in which their forelegs are heading!

Teething

At about this time, the kittens' milk, or deciduous, teeth start to break through the gums. In all, 26 milk teeth – 12 incisors, four canines and 10 premolars (see page 112) – will erupt over the next three weeks or so. From about three months of age, the roots of these first teeth will begin to disappear, the crowns will fall out and 30 new adult, or permanent, teeth will begin to erupt to take their place.

Kittens take their first real steps in week three. They can balance on three legs – to investigate a paw, for instance – even if they do not really know what they are looking at!

THE QUEEN'S INFLUENCES ON HER KITTENS

During the third week of her kittens' lives, the average queen will still be spending about **70** per cent of the day with them. However, she may now leave the kittens on their own for periods of up to one hour at a time.

When the queen is with them, she gives the young kittens the social stimulation that is essential for normal emotional development. Her constant attention speeds up the opening of their eyes if this has not yet occurred (see pages 26–7), and makes them more exploratory and quicker to learn. Hand-reared kittens may not obtain all the stimulation they require, although a devoted human carer can achieve much of what the queen would normally

do. The queen also has an important influence over the kittens' early socialization (see page 31).

It is vital that the queen is well-nourished at this stage, which may not be the case if she is a stray. If a queen is receiving only about **80** per cent of the food that she needs the quality of her milk will be unaffected, but with any less than this the kittens may develop abnormalities due to a shortage of protein when it is most needed for the development of their brains and nervous systems. Male kittens who are malnourished at this stage tend to be abnormally aggressive later, and both males and females may develop into clumsy, poorly co-ordinated cats.

Feeding

To produce enough milk for her kittens, a lactating queen will need to eat more than usual so that she can provide for their nutritional needs as well as her own. Three weeks after giving birth, a mother of four hungry youngsters may need to consume twice the calories that she would normally take in each day (the precise amount of food that she requires will depend on the number of kittens in the litter, their age and the nutritional make-up of her diet).

At this stage the kittens are still entirely dependent on the queen for their nourishment, but – rather than the queen having to encourage them to suck, as she did formerly – the kittens will now initiate more and more of the nursing bouts themselves.

For the first two weeks the kittens identified their mother by her warmth and her smell, but by the end of week three they should begin to recognize her by sight (above).

A three-week-old kitten's body length is 20 cm (8 in).

Week four

As her kittens become more mobile, the queen has to increase her supervision over them and pay greater attention to where they are. If she considers that any of the kittens have strayed too far from the nest, she will try to retrieve them.

The method used for this varies from one queen to another: some will call to their kittens, while others will use their front paws to push stray kittens back to the nest. However, when all else fails, the favoured method employed by most queens involves using their mouths to pick each of the kittens up in turn by the scruff of the neck (see page 26) before dropping them unceremoniously back where they belong.

Finding a new nest-site

The queen may attempt to move her litter to a new nest-site when the kittens are about four weeks old. This is instinctive behaviour, probably designed to prevent the kittens from becoming infested by fleas or other parasites that may imminently hatch out in the original nest (see pages 114–17).

Even though this is obviously unnecessary for a well-cared-for cat, the majority of queens continue to perform this behaviour. However, after spending a day or two in the new location that she has selected,

a queen is usually happy for the litter to be returned to its original site by her owner.

Sensory development

By this fourth week the kittens are able to regulate their own body temperatures. Their senses are also continuing to improve in the following ways.

Balance • This is now well-developed. For instance, if a kitten slips and falls from a height, he can right himself in mid-air in the same way that an adult cat will do, in order to land on his feet.

Sight • The kittens' eyesight is now sufficiently good to enable them to recognize their mother by her appearance rather than by her smell.

Hearing • This is more accurate: the kittens know to approach the calls of their mother and litter mates, but to run away if they hear a growl or a hiss.

Voice • On seeing an unfamiliar cat, the kittens will respond by making hissing sounds and fluffing up their coats in an attempt to make their bodies look bigger. Unfortunately, they are still so small that this appears more comical than threatening.

Gaining independence

The queen will now be preparing the litter of kittens to become more independent of her and ready for weaning (see page 32). If she were wild, she would

A litter-tray must seem a strange object to young kittens at first, but they quickly discover its purpose by watching their mother make use of it. It is unusual for kittens to have problems in learning how to use a litter-tray.

start teaching her kittens how to handle solid food by killing prey animals and bringing them back to the nest to eat in front of the litter.

The queen will also start to demonstrate the use of the litter-tray, and by the end of the fourth week some of the kittens should be using it themselves as they gain voluntary control of urination and defecation. For some reason, most kittens go through a brief phase of trying to eat the litter, but soon discover its real purpose by imitating their mother. Brought up in the correct environment, kittens are very easy to toilet-train (see pages 74–7).

SOCIALIZATION

Kittens benefit from careful handling as soon as their eyes open, but are most receptive to being socialized between the fourth and seventh weeks of their lives. Their experiences during this period will have lasting effects on their personalities and on the way in which they react to people and other animals.

This is the time when kittens learn their identity. This means that those kittens who have been hand-reared from their birth and kept isolated from other cats will never fully learn that they *are* cats. As a result, they will react aggressively or defensively when they do meet other members of their own species.

Human contact

If all the handling comes from only one person, the kittens may become over-attached to that person and suspicious of everyone else. It is therefore best if they have early experience of all kinds of people, including children as well as adult men and women.

At first, gentle stroking and talking are the best ways to socialize young kittens. As they grow older, this can be backed up by interactive play with toys.

From four weeks onwards, kittens should be handled gently for at least one hour every day. Even at this age, the kittens may have very different characters: some of them are already more adventurous than others.

The queen's behaviour

The queen's reactions to people will influence her kittens' behaviour. If she is very wary, it will therefore be better for her to be separated temporarily from the kittens when they are being socialized and handled.

THE PURPOSE OF SOCIALIZATION

Domestic kittens have a much longer socialization period than that of cats in the wild, and this allows them to become socialized to several species at once. The most important species is, of course, man.

Recent research has shown that at least one hour per day of sensitive handling and other friendly contact is needed to maximize a kitten's potential to be friendly towards people. Less human contact than this will produce a kitten who is nervous of people for the first year of his life, while little or no handling will result in a kitten who needs taming as if he were a wild animal.

A four-week-old kitten's body length is 21 cm (8½ in).

Weeks five and six

Until the fifth week, the kittens have been unable to perceive distance, and appear to have experienced difficulty in telling vertical and horizontal surfaces apart by their appearance alone. They also often failed to make the connection between what an object looked like and where it was, with the result that they frequently blundered into any obstructions in the vicinity of the nest.

However, by the end of the fifth week the kittens' visual abilities will be almost completely mature, and they should also have learned more about the appearance of their bodies. Four-week-old kittens tend to behave as if they do not know what their own paws look like!

WEANING

During the fourth week, the kittens rather than the queen would have taken the initiative in starting bouts of sucking. By the fifth week, the queen will begin to prevent this by keeping out of the kittens' way, or by lying on her belly to prevent their access to her teats.

This may appear cruel, but in the wild it would be essential to the queen's survival, as providing the litter of growing kittens with enough milk will now be placing severe strains on her vital body reserves. If she were having to hunt as well, she could be losing up to 6 g (¼ oz) per day in weight for each kitten being fed.

FEEDING A LARGE LITTER

A large litter will place the queen under much greater strain than a small one, and this will be reflected in her kittens' body weights. For instance, kittens in a litter of eight are about 25 per cent lighter at five weeks of age than those with only one sibling. The queen has to decide when to begin persuading her kittens to take solid food. If she leaves this too late, she will run the risk of sacrificing so much of herself to provide milk that she may be too weak to become pregnant again.

When she feels that the time is right, the queen will attempt to speed up weaning by restricting the amount of milk that her kittens can obtain. This is usually effective in a few days, and she can then relax and resume her normal relationship with her litter.

Energetic kittens soon become hungry, and require little encouragement to fill up with solid rather than liquid fuel.

Moving on to solid food

By the beginning of the sixth week, the kittens should be taking at least some solid food, although they will still be sucking milk regularly from their mother.

If the family were living in the wild, the queen would now be bringing back half-killed prey – rather than dead animals (see pages 30–1) – for her kittens, in order to build up their skills for the moment when they would have to start hunting for themselves.

A five-week-old kitten's body length is 22.5 cm (9 in).

When five- and six-week-old kittens begin to play, they find each other much more fun than any toys that may be offered to them.

Starting to play

With their improvement in vision and co-ordination, the kittens begin to play together in earnest. They still pay little attention to toys, and initially their games are just a rough-and-tumble: more sophisticated play will develop in the seventh and eighth weeks.

A six-week-old kitten's body length is 24 cm (9½ in).

Imitating the queen

The kittens pay a lot of attention to their mother at this age. They will imitate her in the kinds of food that she eats, as well as in how far she will climb up furniture or other objects. The queen's reactions to people will continue to affect the ease with which the kittens are socialized themselves (see page 31).

Unless it is unavoidable for some reason, kittens should not go to their future homes for at least another two weeks. If they are separated from their mother and litter mates as early as the sixth week, they will tend to become fearful, aggressive and slow to learn.

The gape response

It is during the sixth week that the kittens' so called gape response first appears. Adult cats typically show this when sniffing at scents left by other cats. In this reaction, the lower jaw drops and the cat assumes an expression of extreme concentration for a few seconds.

What is actually happening is that air containing the interesting scent is being drawn into the nose, as well as into a second set of smell sensors called the vomeronasal organ. This is located just above the roof of the mouth, and is connected to it by a pair of tiny tubes opening just behind the front teeth. The vomeronasal organ is found in cats, dogs and many other mammals, but not in humans.

Weeks seven and eight

As they reach the end of the socialization period in their seventh week, kittens begin to behave more like young cats. Their sleep assumes the adult pattern of quiet, shallow periods between bouts of 'twitchy' dreaming sleep. They now have a full set of milk teeth (see page 112) and can both walk and run with ease, so that their exploratory play becomes much more daring than before. Kittens spend a great deal of their time playing in the seventh and eighth weeks, and this activity includes mock-fighting between the litter mates, chasing behaviour and pouncing on toys.

Play-fighting seems to be as much fun for kittens as it is entertaining to watch. Rarely do these mock bouts turn into real fights.

Play-fighting

The play-fights between kittens have now become ritualized encounters. These incorporate special postures and actions reserved exclusively for play, and include the following.

The side-step • In this action a kitten moves along sideways like a crab, with an arched back.

The face-off • This involves the kitten waving one front paw while swishing his tail.

The vertical stance • In this posture, the kitten stands upright on his hindlegs.

All these actions are virtually guaranteed to persuade a litter mate to start a game. Occasionally such games do turn into real fights, but the kittens learn to indicate when they are only playing by keeping their mouths half-open (in the so-called 'play-face'), and by not growling or emitting any other aggressive sounds.

WHY DO KITTENS PLAY?

The reasons why kittens play so much are not fully understood. It is thought that they may use play as a preparation for hunting, especially as play contains so many elements that resemble predatory behaviour. It is unlikely that play uses up 'surplus' energy, as it only adds about 4 per cent to the amount of food that the kittens need. Moreover, kittens whose mothers are short of milk — and who may therefore need to hunt for themselves sooner rather than later — actually play more than kittens who are fully fed.

Play with their litter mates probably also enhances the kittens' competitive and social abilities, so that they will know how to cope with meeting other cats when they begin to venture outdoors.

A seven-week-old kitten's body length is 27.5 cm (11 in).

Games with toys

These types of games are not usually very common until the seventh week, and even then are fairly limited. However, by the time the kittens are eight weeks old they will be going through a full range of prey-catching actions with toys, including pouncing, striking them with their paws, and holding them in their mouths and biting them. The kittens will also hold larger toys in their front paws while raking at them with their hind claws.

Male kittens often tend to be more energetic than females at 'hunting' toys.

The fear/avoidance response

At the end of the eighth week, many kittens will begin to show a fearful reaction towards other animals or people whom they have not already encountered in the first weeks of their lives.

If this response is fairly mild, it can generally be overcome by careful exposure to what is unfamiliar within the next few weeks. However, a kitten who is especially fearful of people will need a great deal of dedication on the part of his new owner – and more than a little luck – in order to develop into a happy, confident and rewarding pet.

By the time that kittens are ready to go to their new homes at the age of eight weeks, they have discovered the full pleasure of playing with toys and many other interesting objects.

An eight-week-old kitten's body length is 30 cm (12 in).

From eight weeks to one year

It is customary for non-pedigree kittens to be moved to their new homes at about eight weeks of age, while pedigree kittens are often not separated from their litters for re-homing until four or five weeks later.

Physical maturity

By 10 weeks, the kittens will have reached between one-quarter and one-third of their adult body weights. At about this point, male kittens begin to grow faster than females. The following physical changes will also take place during this period.

Sight • By 10 weeks of age, the kittens' vision will be 16 times more acute than it was when they were three weeks old. The irises in their eyeballs will also have begun to darken into their adult colour.

Coat colour • Also by the age of 10 weeks, the kittens' final coat pattern will be visible. However, long-haired cats do not achieve their adult coats until after their first moult (see page 109).

Teeth • The kittens' milk teeth will be shed and then replaced by a set of permanent adult teeth when the kittens are between three and six months old.

The chart below shows the expected growth curve for a normal healthy male and female kitten. At 10 weeks, the male begins to grow significantly faster than the female.

A kitten must not be allowed outdoors until one week after his first vaccinations (see pages 120–1), but when that time comes he should begin to explore his new world in earnest.

Sexual maturity

This is reached when kittens are about seven months old (this occurs earlier in the Siamese cat; later in the Persian). If they remain unneutered, male kittens will achieve adult weights up to 50 per cent greater than if they were castrated (see page 122).

Re-homing

Recent research has demonstrated that some aspects of a kitten's 'personality' change a great deal in the period when he first moves to a new home, probably as a result of his having to adapt to his new surroundings.

Once he has been re-homed, the kitten will begin to transfer his former attachment to his mother and litter mates to his new owner. Feeding will help to cement the bond between kitten and owner, but other activities – such as stroking, talking and playing – are also important.

A kitten is at his most playful when he is 10 to 14 weeks old, and male kittens in particular are at their most interactive at this stage.

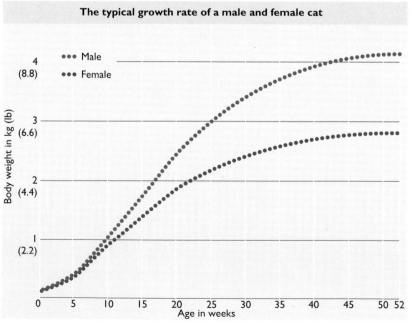

The typical growth rate of a male and female cat

••• Male
••• Female

Body weight in kg (lb)

4 (8.8)
3 (6.6)
2 (4.4)
1 (2.2)

0   5   10   15   20   25   30   35   40   45   50 52
Age in weeks

Games with a kitten's new owners at this time are both rewarding and an aid to forming a lasting relationship.

Social skills

These should be built up as soon as possible after re-homing, by introducing a kitten to a wide range of experiences, including unfamiliar people, dogs and even car journeys. His initial reactions will be strongly influenced by the events to which he was exposed up to the age of seven weeks (see page 31). It is important to remember that kittens who are nervous of anything new at nine weeks old are likely to continue to react in this way, unless treated carefully and with patience.

Good human-cat relationships are based on mutual trust. A kitten who has been handled gently by all kinds of people, including children, from four weeks onwards should be well-prepared for family life when he is re-homed at eight weeks.

FERAL FAMILIES

If a kitten stays with his mother and litter mates after the age of 12 weeks – as he would do in the wild – he will become increasingly self-reliant as far as food is concerned, and could be totally independent of his mother by the time he is five months old.

Feral male kittens who remain with their litters start to become more aggressive in their social play from four months onwards. They also begin to exhibit sexual behaviour – for example, using their mouths to grasp females by the scruff – at five months. At about six months old they almost always leave their family groups, and may roam freely for several months before finding a territory of their own.

Females, on the other hand, may stay with their mothers if there is enough food for all, and will then share the chores of rearing kittens in future years.

Understanding cats

Pet cats are often thought of as loners because of their tendency towards aloof and independent behaviour, but no pet cat is truly alone. At the very least an individual will share a home territory with his owner, and if he is allowed to roam outdoors he is likely to interact with other cats.

All cats are socially active, and over millions of years of evolution they have developed a number of ways of communicating with each other.

Communicating with your kitten

There may soon be a kitten in your life. He will see you as an all-powerful guardian angel who provides shelter, warmth, food and company. Although you are not a cat, he will assume that you are able to understand him.

By learning in advance something of the methods of communication used by cats, you should avoid any frustrating communication crises when your kitten comes to live with you. Some of the body postures and expressions commonly used by cats, and the sounds that they make, are still not fully understood, but with practice and experience you should be able to make sense of your kitten's basic body language. In time, you should become more and more sensitive to his feelings, and your relationship with him will become stronger and more enjoyable as a result.

This kitten is frightened: his arched back may be a sign that he cannot decide whether to attack or defend himself. Kittens also often arch their backs when playing together.

BODY LANGUAGE

By adopting certain postures, facial expressions and behaviour, many animals – including ourselves – can communicate their moods to others of their kind. Smiling, hand-shaking and kissing are all elements of human body language that do not require clarification with words. However, we rely so heavily on both the written and spoken word to communicate that we are less good at picking up subtle body-language signals.

Cats are different: they use body language as one of their main communication methods at short range, and they are 'pre-programmed' from birth to be highly skilled and perceptive observers of the way that other animals look and behave.

When interacting with a cat and trying to interpret his mood or intentions, it is important to look at his whole body to get an overall picture of how he feels. However, it is not as easy to interpret a cat's body language as you might think. Although there are a number of individual and characteristic body postures and facial expressions, cats also often adopt particular combinations of these that they understand, but that we do not. Future scientific studies may reveal more of the hidden secrets of cat body language.

Body postures

During an aggressive interaction with a cat or another animal, an attacking cat will generally try to make his body appear as large as possible by standing fully upright. He may also erect the fur along his back.

By contrast, a very submissive cat will crouch down low to the ground and tuck his head into his shoulders in an attempt to look as unthreatening as possible. If he is pushed, however, he may launch a defensive onslaught on his attacker from that position.

An arched-back posture is thought to be typical of a cat who is frightened, or who cannot decide whether to attack or defend. It is also a body posture that is commonly used in play between kittens.

Facial expressions

Judging a cat's mood from his facial expression can be difficult, as this relies on an interpretation of many factors including the direction of his stare, the size and shape of his pupils and the way he is holding his ear flaps. What makes it even more tricky is that he may be constantly making subtle alterations to his facial expression as his mood changes.

With his tail held up high, ears pricked forwards and pupils narrowed, this cat is demonstrating that he is in a friendly and approachable state of mind.

Ears held flat against the side of his head, wide circular pupils, an arched back and a tail held erect are all signs that this cat is frightened but may be unsure whether to attack or defend.

This cat is behaving aggressively and is warning that he may attack. His ears are pulled backwards, his pupils are narrow slits and his tail is limp.

A relaxed cat who is keeping himself to himself will look alert, but will hold his tail limply.

In general, a submissive cat will avoid direct eye-contact with an aggressor, and will fold down his ear flaps so that they lie against the side of his head. His pupils are likely to be dilated. The aggressor's ear flaps will be erect but rotated towards the side, so that more of the back side of each flap is visible from the front.

Use of the tail tip

A cat uses his tail primarily as a balance aid when he is jumping, climbing and galloping, but he can also use it as a communication tool when he is stationary. The tip of the tail can move independently of the base, and tail-tip 'twitches' are familiar to all observers of cat behaviour. Despite what you may have read or heard, however, these movements have not been adequately studied and no-one really understands their meaning.

Whole-tail positions

These are better understood. During greetings and play, a cat will normally hold his tail erect. An arched tail is typical of a cat who is defensively aggressive, while his attacker will hold his tail low, although not between his hindlegs. Tail-swishing may indicate arousal, anger or annoyance.

Clawing and scratching

A cat may claw and scratch at objects for any of the following reasons.
• To create a very visible sign of his presence.
• The marks may attract other cats to investigate the scents that have been deposited by special glands on the cat's feet.
• To keep his claws in good condition.
• As an active way of signalling his dominance over subordinate spectators.
• As an indication of excitement during interactions with people.

Feral and farm cats, as well as pet cats, indulge in clawing and scratching at certain objects. Outdoors, these may include a range of wooden surfaces such as logs, fence-posts and trees; indoors, carpets, furniture and door frames may be clawed. Luckily, most cats can be trained to use a designated scratching post placed strategically inside the house (see page 82).

Touch

A kitten's sense of touch is the most developed of all his senses at birth: in fact, this sense is present even in a 28-day-old foetus (see page 15). As a result, tactile communication is important to kittens, but it is also a feature of adult-cat behaviour.

Cats commonly rub their heads and bodies against other animals and inanimate objects. This behaviour may be involved in transferring scent messages to other cats: such messages are used to signal a cat's earlier presence in a particular place. Head- and body-rubbing may also be used to reinforce social status, as a cat who feels subordinate will head-rub what he considers to be a more dominant animal. And that should include his owner!

CAT CALLS

Some adult cats, particularly of certain breeds such as the Siamese, are very vocal animals. Scientists have identified 11 distinct cat vocalizations, but there may in fact be an infinite number of cat calls, as individuals seem to adapt and personalize standard calls.

Purring

A cat's purr is produced by his vocal cords and the muscles of his larynx. Although purring is one of the most familiar of all cat sounds, experts are still unsure why cats do it. The current view is that purring is associated with actual or desired contact with other cats or people. Cats may start to purr in any or all of the following circumstances.
• In their owners' presence.
• When nursing kittens.

When a cat head-rubs his owner in this way, he may be exchanging scents, as well as confirming that he accepts his submissive role in the relationship.

• When greeting familiar cat friends.
• When rubbing and rolling.
• During drowsy sleep.
• In warm, familiar environments.
• When in extreme pain.

Miaowing

The fact that there are reported to be 31 alternative spellings of this vocalization indicates not only the subtle differences in the sounds, but also the varying ways in which we interpret them.

Some cats develop specific kinds of miaow for use in different circumstances. For instance, a cat may use one miaow during food-begging, and another when he wants his cat flap opened. Certain cats also engage in 'silent' miaowing, when their mouths go through the actions but no sound is produced. As with so many vocalizations, the purpose of this is not understood.

Growls and yowls

Cats produce a range of sounds associated with sexual and aggressive activity. A queen in heat produces a characteristic call (see page 12), while competing tom cats produce aggressive growls and yowls. Hissing is used as a warning of imminent attack.

Kitten calls

Newborn kittens are not able to produce the full range of adult-cat calls: their personal repertoire of sounds develops as they grow older. Kittens cannot hear at birth (see page 25), and so their first distress calls are 'pre-programmed' and do not need to be learned. A kitten of a few days old can also purr, and will do so when his mother suckles him. First miaows appear around the time of weaning. At about the same stage, a kitten will develop aggressive vocalizations such as growls and yowls. Kittens do not normally hiss until the age of five weeks.

INTERACTING WITH CATS

When interacting with cats, it is important to remember that they tend to be independent characters who prefer any relationship to be handled on their terms. Much of their body language is geared around 'go-away' signals: for instance, rather than looking at you to see if you are friendly, a strange cat will judge you by how threatening you appear.

CAT PSYCHOLOGY

Have you noticed how, when confronted with a group of new people, a cat will home in on the one person who does not like cats? The reason is simple. As soon as a cat enters a room, the cat-lovers will stare at him and focus all their efforts on trying to attract his attention. They will talk, begin to move about and may ultimately lunge forward to try to touch him.

In contrast, the person who does not care for cats is likely to remain calm and quiet, and will probably avoid eye-contact with the cat from the misplaced fear that staring will attract his attention. All of these actions will indicate to the cat that this person is more friendly and less of a threat than the others. Much to that person's annoyance, the cat will therefore tend to seek closer contact.

Making friends

When trying to make the acquaintance of a cat, it is best to sit calmly and to ignore him. Speak in a quiet voice. If you do look at him, concentrate on his tail rather than on his face. The cat may remain some distance away at first, or he may approach you. In either case, avoid making any sudden movements, and let him explore you with his eyes, ears and nose.

If the cat sniffs you and then slowly walks off to lie down a little way away from you, you should take his behaviour as a compliment: if he considered you to be a threat, he would not even have come close to you.

If he decides to sit in your lap, head-rub you, purr and tread up and down with his front feet, you should consider yourself very special indeed.

Given time and a complete absence of manhandling, even cats who at first seem very unfriendly may warm to people who adopt this kind of approach.

Learning about cats

You may be planning to take on a new kitten in the near future, but have little or no previous experience of cats. In this case, it will be helpful if you are able to spend time beforehand watching and interacting with cats owned by friends, neighbours and relatives.

Every cat has his own personality, and all the cats whom you meet are likely to respond to you in quite different ways. Handle the cats, and ask their owners if you can help with health-checks (see pages 106–7) or grooming (see pages 108–11).

The more time that you spend with cats before you obtain your own kitten, the more likely it is that you will be 'cat-friendly' by the time you go to collect him.

Cat-handling tips

• Never chase after a cat in order to get hold of him: he will fear for his life.
• When carrying out procedures such as grooming, tooth-cleaning or administering medicines, restrain a cat firmly and confidently. Cats do not like being restrained, but quickly become resigned to their fate if they are held properly. They tend to become anxious and distressed if they are restrained either too firmly or not firmly enough.
• If you are handling a cat who is struggling – even playfully – avoid letting him go (if possible) until he is calm. If the cat is allowed to believe that struggling in this way will result in his release, he may quickly become difficult to handle.
• Hand-feeding tiny amounts of food is a good way of winning the confidence of a shy cat. He may not take food from your fingers at first, so you may have to drop it on the ground until he trusts you.
• Always be gentle when stroking a cat, and avoid rubbing his belly: many cats see this as a vulnerable part of their anatomy, and will try to protect it.
• Although some cats become calm when cradled on their backs, most prefer to remain the right way up.

You should adopt an appropriate degree of restraint when handling a cat to carry out a procedure. He will be easier to control if he is in unfamiliar territory, such as on a table top.

Preparing for a new kitten

Becoming a cat-owner involves major new responsibilities and requires total commitment. Getting ready for the arrival of a kitten also takes time, so you should start in advance. You will find advice here on choosing the right kind of cat for your family, preparing your home and planning your kitten's diet.

What makes a good owner?

Some people believe that any cat-lover can care for a cat, but affection alone will not keep a kitten fit and healthy. Equally, however, it is not essential to have a big bank balance and a large house and garden. What you do need is commitment: you must be willing to put your kitten first, and to make sacrifices for him.

No matter what kind of kitten you may choose, or how independent a lifestyle he may have, he will still

The kitten whom you adopt will become a member of your family, and will rely on you to care for him throughout his life. Some cats have been known to live for 30 years!

be dependent on you for his nourishment, education, shelter, protection and healthcare. The following points and questions should help you to decide whether you have what it takes to care for a kitten properly.

Preparations

Your house and garden may need to be adapted to accommodate your kitten's needs (see pages 50–1), and there will be a number of cat-care items to buy (see pages 52–3). Do you have the money to spend?

Food

Far from being just another mouth to feed, your kitten will have special nutritional needs. Despite the wide availability of prepared cat foods, you will have to think very carefully about how to satisfy his dietary requirements (see pages 54–67): it takes more than the ability to use a tin-opener to feed a cat properly.

Education

Cats are born with the instincts of free-living wild animals, and your kitten will need your help in

---

THINKING AHEAD

Your kitten may well live for 10 years or more, and your life could change dramatically in that time. How will your cat fit into your plans? What would happen if you had to move house, possibly abroad? Think about possibilities that you would perhaps prefer to ignore, such as sudden long-term illness, disability or death. What will happen to your cat? You will have to make provision for him. Your responsibility to him is for life — and that means his life, not yours.

adjusting to a human lifestyle. When you collect him at the age of about eight weeks (see page 36) he should already have learned a lot about being a cat, and about the houses that we live in and the sometimes strange things that humans do. You will not need to train your kitten to sit, come and stay in the same way as a young puppy, but he must learn from you what is acceptable behaviour and what is not (see page 50).

Exercise

Cats spend more time sleeping each day than many other animals, but they require physical and mental exercise to stay healthy. You will need to provide your kitten with games and furnishings to stimulate both his body and his brain (see pages 82–5), especially if you plan to keep him indoors or to give him limited access outside in a suitable enclosure (see pages 88–9).

Healthcare

Cats do not just stay healthy – you have to keep them that way. They need regular vaccinations, parasite control, dental care and grooming. You can undertake some of these tasks at home yourself; others will need to be carried out at a vet centre (see pages 102–3).

Medical care for cats is very sophisticated, and can be expensive. Accidents and illness can happen at any time, and some cats develop long-term problems that need years of treatment. Could you cope with the costs of unexpected medical care, or with the cost of taking out health insurance for your kitten (see page 105)?

Holidays

It is unlikely that you will take your kitten on holiday with you. Who will look after him?

Your family

Even if you plan to be entirely responsible for caring for your new kitten, he will still interact with the other members of your family. Do they all like cats as much as you do? Or, although you may be desperate to own a kitten, are you in the minority?

Inevitably, especially while learning the rules, your kitten will damage your property. How will you and your family react if he decides to 'territory-mark' your new sofa with his claws? Will you all accept with good humour odd hairs in your food when he is moulting? What about muddy paw prints on your clothes, the carpets and the furniture when he dashes in through his cat flap on a wet day?

Finances

You may be able to afford to keep a cat now, but what if your circumstances were suddenly to change? Would you make sacrifices elsewhere in your life?

Other useful checkpoints

• Talk to cat-owning friends, who will give you their honest opinions on the advantages and disadvantages of cat-ownership.
• There is nothing like first-hand experience, so, when cat-owning friends go away, offer to look after their cat for them (ideally, this should be in their own home).
• Prepare a mock budget by making a list of all the items that you need to set yourself up as a cat-owner (see pages 52–3). Then work out the 'running costs' of a typical cat, including his food, parasite-control products, vaccinations, healthcare and health insurance (see page 105), cattery fees, replacement costs for worn-out toys and, of course, presents!

One of the most important decisions that you will need to make is whether to take on one kitten or two (see pages 46–7).

Making the right choice

Deciding on the type of kitten that will suit you best can be a difficult task, as there are so many cats – varying greatly in appearance and, to some degree, in temperament – from which to choose. You may well already be attracted to a breed or type of cat because of its looks, but you must also consider its behavioural quirks as well as any special care needs it may have. For instance, Siamese cats are beautiful but generally vociferous animals, while long-haired cats require much more hair-care than their short-coated cousins.

Having answered the basic questions about owning a cat (see pages 42–3), your aim should be to carry out some research to find out more about all the different types of cat that are available. Now is also the time to decide whether you would like one kitten or two, what sex your kitten will be and whether you would prefer a young or an older kitten (see page 47).

The different types of cat that are available can be divided into the following groups.

Pure-bred kittens

The advantage of choosing a pure-bred kitten is that you will have a good idea of how he will look – and to some extent what kind of temperament he will have – when he is an adult. He should turn out to be similar in these respects to his parents, his grandparents and even his great-grandparents: that is what makes a pure-bred cat what he is.

Cross-bred kittens

A kitten is described as cross-bred if both his parents were pure breeds but of different types. New breeds of cat are usually 'man-made' by breeding similar-looking cross-bred cats together for many generations, until it is predictable that the kittens in a litter and their parents will resemble each other. However, the mysteries of genetics are such that there are no guarantees that a cross-bred kitten will resemble one of his parents more than the other.

Moggies

A kitten may be called a moggie if one or both of his parents are cross-breds (or moggies) themselves. With a moggie kitten, it can be difficult to predict exactly how big he will be, what he will look like or what kind of character he will have when he is fully grown, as his parentage may have been continually mixed over several generations.

THE PURE BREEDS

There are various systems for classifying and grouping pure-bred cats. Unfortunately, there has been little or no research into the characteristic temperaments of different breeds, and, as a result, breed descriptions tend to give cats almost human personality traits and are based on subjective opinions. Such descriptions may still be of great use to you in your research, but their possible bias is worth bearing in mind.

The following classifications and breed notes are based on the views of the editor of one of the UK's top cat magazines.

There are two distinct body types among pure-bred cats. One is 'cobby', with a roundish head and broad shoulders (examples are the Persian and the British shorthair). The other type is lithe and muscular, with a narrow head (the Siamese is a typical example). Additional breeds fall between these two extremes.

Pure-bred cats may be grouped depending on the length of their hair-coat into longhairs, semi-longhairs and shorthairs. The following are just a few examples.

Longhairs

Many people are attracted to these cats because of their stunning looks. They are undoubtedly very impressive, but when thinking about a long-haired kitten you must be practical. These cats do require considerable owner-effort – particularly when it comes to their hair-care – to remain good-looking and healthy. For those people who love them, doing what is necessary is all part of the pleasure of owning a cat like this. But do you have the time and the inclination? Think about this carefully, and speak to long-haired-cat owners before you make a decision.

A Peke-faced Persian.

All too often in my surgery, I see cats with matted coats and skin disorders brought in for procedures such as vaccination. Many of their owners have failed them, and are shocked when I point out that their cats are suffering through neglect.

Persians • These are the most popular of the long-haired breeds. They are available in an abundance of colours and patterns, and generally have placid natures, although the colourpoints (originally Persians crossed with Siamese cats) have a slightly more lively nature and tend to be more vocal. Persians will happily take to life as indoor cats. They get on well with other cats (although it is not a good idea to combine a Persian with a very boisterous breed), other animals and children.

A Norwegian forest cat.

Semi-longhairs

This description includes a small group of attractive breeds which have long, soft coats that are easier to maintain than the full coat of the Persian. Some are closely related to short-haired breeds.

Balinese cats • These could be described as long-haired versions of Siamese cats, and have the same colourpoints on their faces, ears, legs and tails. However, their temperament is less boisterous, although they are equally intelligent.

Ragdoll cats • These have become very popular over recent years. They are large, attractive cats with lively and affectionate natures. They come in several coat patterns, including colourpoint and bi-colour. These playful cats are well-suited to life indoors.

Birmans • These are beautifully marked cats. They have dark colourpoints on their faces, ears, legs (always with white paws) and tails. Their china-blue eyes are particularly striking. Intelligent and lively, they have a quiet charm and mix well with children and other animals.

Norwegian forest and Maine coon cats•
These fairly large, athletic breeds have recently become very popular. They are hardy, active cats who appreciate the great outdoors and prefer to be independent. Both breeds have pleasant natures, and come in a range of colours and patterns.

Turkish vans • These charming cats have a distinct appearance: white with auburn or cream markings on the face, around and below the ears, and a tail ringed in two shades of auburn. Their coats are soft and silky. Turkish vans are intelligent and, though slow to mature, they grow into large cats. They like water, and some actively enjoy swimming.

Somalis • These long-haired versions of Abyssinians (see page 46) are similar in colouring and have a lithe body shape, although they are a little less energetic and athletic. However, they are playful and enjoy releasing their energy outdoors. Somalis are quiet, sensitive and affectionate.

Shorthairs

This simple coat description encompasses a very wide range of different breeds.

British shorthairs • These cats are strong and sturdy. They are available in a broad spectrum of colours and patterns, from self-solid colours to colourpoint, and everything in between. Their coats are short and dense. They are active, hardy and long-lived, and often grow into big cats with appetites to match. British shorthairs are intelligent cats and make companionable pets. They enjoy fresh air and sunshine, and so will appreciate access to a safe garden. Many are keen hunters, so their owners should expect regular gifts!

Oriental shorthairs • These cats have a long, slender body shape. They are among the most intelligent and energetic of cat breeds and make the liveliest of pets, guaranteed to keep owners on their toes. They demand a great deal of attention, and their distinctive voice will ensure that they are not ignored. Mischievous and also easily bored, oriental shorthairs are

A British shorthair.

perhaps best-suited to living with other cats and to having plenty of human company. If raised to it from kittenhood, they make ideal indoor pets. They come in a wide range of colours.

Siamese cats • These form one of the best-known of all the cat breeds. Long and slender in build, Siamese cats are intelligent and vocal. They are confident creatures and will live happily alongside other animals, but can tend to want to dominate the whole household. They expect to receive plenty of attention, but reward their owners by becoming devoted pets. Well-bred and well-kept Siamese cats are healthy, hardy and long-lived. They come in a wide range of colourpoints.

Burmese cats • These are playful extroverts who like to be involved in whatever is going on. They usually have plenty of energy, and are fond of climbing. Often muscular and sturdy, Burmese cats have short, easy-to-care-for, glossy coats.

Abyssinians • These are distinctive, wild-looking cats, whose ticked coats (each hair bears two to three dark bands) set them apart from other breeds. Abyssinians are intelligent and inquisitive, with a taste for adventure. At the same time, they are affectionate and enjoy their home comforts. They are also sociable with other cats.

Russian blues • These are beautiful grey cats with vivid green, almond-shaped eyes and dense, silky coats that have a glossy sheen. They are gentle, affectionate and undemanding cats.

Korats • These cats come from Thailand, and are grey in colour. They have heart-shaped faces and large eyes, and a light silver tipping gives their coats a sparkle. They are playful and lively.

New breeds

The following are all breeds that have been developed over recent years.

Asians • These are Burmese-type cats. They come in a selection of striking colours, including ticked tabby. Asians are sturdy cats, and are full of character.

Ocicats • These cats have a wild, spotted appearance. Medium to large in build, they are distantly related to the Siamese and Abyssinian breeds. Ocicats are sociable and can become devoted to their owners.

Bengal cats • Owning one of these cats is the nearest thing to having a leopard in your living-room. Their luxuriant, golden-spotted coats are described as pelts, and their wild looks and build belie their pussycat natures. They are large and sociable pets, who enjoy family life and the great outdoors.

A Bengal cat.

OTHER CONSIDERATIONS

Just from the examples given, it should be obvious that a comprehensive study of the different cat breeds is essential if you are to identify the right kind of kitten for you and your family. The golden rule to remember is that looks are not everything. Books on cat breeds will give you an idea of typical characteristics but, as I have already mentioned, they can be misleading.

Carry out additional research by talking to people who live and work with cats of all kinds. Ask the opinions of your vet and the nurses at your vet centre, and speak to other owners, animal-behaviour experts and even professional groomers. They will all have interesting and valid views on this important subject.

One kitten or two?

If you are concerned about the amount of time that your kitten will spend alone, you may think about obtaining two kittens. However, this is not a valid solution, as another cat will be no substitute for you.

Cats are very socially adaptable. If there is enough food and space for both of them, two cats may live very happily together, but your relationship with them may be different to the relationship that you might have with just one kitten.

At first, as they are both the same kind of animal and 'speak' the same language, the two kittens may bond with each other more strongly than they will with you. However, as they grow older they may begin to challenge each other for the position of top cat in your household, especially if they are males. If they are different sexes, they will try to mate if they are not neutered sufficiently early (see pages 122–3).

Contrary to what some people say, two cats are not less trouble than one. Having said this, many owners believe that some breeds – the Cornish Rex is one example (see below) – are happier when kept in pairs. If you do take on two kittens, remember that you are taking on twice the cost and twice the responsibility. Choose two kittens from the same litter who seem to get on well: some kittens are obvious loners. Make sure that you neuter them at the earliest opportunity, especially if they are both males or of different sexes.

Male or female?

Adult male, unneutered cats are stocky and thickset, and are usually more active and destructive than females. They tend to roam, urine-mark to notify other cats of their presence, and to defend large territories. As a result, they are often involved in fights with other cats. Neutering male cats is the best way of helping to control this macho behaviour (see page 122).

On first meeting a cat who has been neutered before puberty, it can be difficult to be sure from the outward appearance or behaviour whether the cat is male or female. This is because neutered males tend to behave more like females (for example, females are generally more affectionate towards their owners than entire male cats). The characteristics of the different sexes, and the question of whether you plan to neuter your kitten, should play a part in your decision.

Young or old?

The best age to bring home a kitten is when he is eight weeks old (see page 36), but you may perhaps wish to consider taking on a well-socialized older kitten of six to 12 months old, such as one who is available from an animal-rescue centre.

If the kitten is pure-bred, the same considerations about his temperament should apply as to choosing a kitten from a litter (see pages 68–9). In my opinion, taking on a young kitten is really the best option for most families with no cat-owning experience, as it is both fun and educational to witness the development of a young kitten into an adult cat.

CURLY-COATED CATS

Two breeds stand out on their own for having soft, short, wavy coats. Devon and Cornish Rex cats seem to moult less than other breeds, and some people who are allergic to cat hair have found that they can live with them without problems. Both breeds are available in a wide range of colours.

DEVON REX (right)
These small, lightly built cats have shorter coats than their Cornish cousins. Their faces have a distinctive 'pixie' appearance, with large eyes and ears, and short, wedge-shaped muzzles. They are very active and playful, and need plenty of attention and stimulation.

CORNISH REX
This is the larger of the two breeds. These cats are fairly solid, and have long legs and long, tapering tails. They are intelligent and lively with a sense of fun and an ability to climb, so are not for the faint-hearted. They are happiest when kept in pairs, and appreciate plenty of human attention.

Finding a kitten

Once you have decided on the type of cat that you would like, you can start looking for possible sources of a suitable kitten.

If you wish to obtain an eight-week-old, pure-bred kitten from a litter, your first aim should be to find the right breeding queen. In temperament as well as in appearance, she should be exactly the sort of cat you are hoping to own yourself.

If you would like a cross-bred or moggie kitten of the same age, you may not have to wait for very long. However, as most queens only come into heat during the spring and summer (see page 123), kittens are not in abundance all year round. Most matings between different breeds or cross-breeds of cat are unplanned, so you are unlikely to be able to choose the mother before she becomes pregnant; you are far more likely to see the litter of kittens and the queen together.

It is wise to avoid taking children on these initial visits to see litters, as they may be very disappointed if you decide that a particular queen, her kittens or their environment are unsuitable in any way. Carrying out a proper search will take time and effort.

A PURE-BRED KITTEN
Where to start

• Contact the national cat club of your chosen breed (look in cat magazines or ask at a local vet centre for a contact telephone number). The club should be able to put you in touch with breeders in your area and beyond.
• Visit local and even national cat shows: you will make useful

---

WARNING

Do not even consider obtaining a kitten from a pet shop or another outlet that claims to sell a range of different breeds. In my view, such places are totally unsuitable environments for kittens to live in even for a short period, and any kittens sold from them are likely to have had a very bad start in life.

---

contacts here, and you will be able to talk to breeders and meet their cats.
• If you have a friend who owns a cat of the breed that you like, find out where the cat came from. If possible, take a note of his pedigree and parents' names in case you come across them again.
• Look in local newspapers. Many people who own pregnant queens advertise litters before they are born.

What to do next

• Make a shortlist of breeders with suitable queens and arrange to visit them all. Try to find out which toms the breeders have chosen to mate with the queens in whom you are interested, and visit them if you can.
• When you go to see a queen, take a long, hard look not just at her, but at her owner and the environment in which your kitten would be brought up. Remember that a kitten's early experiences will have a significant influence on his mental development (see page 31), so you should get a good impression of how he will be treated in his early weeks of life.

Planning for the adoption of a kitten is a project that will benefit from the input of the whole family. If well-organized, the process can also be a very educational one for children.

If you are an inexperienced owner you should try to ensure that your kitten will stay with his litter until you collect him, and that he has been well-socialized to people (see page 31).

• It may seem more convenient to obtain your kitten from a friend than to carry out a proper search, but do not do so because it is an easy option. You can compromise on looks, but never on temperament.

• Avoid restricting your search for breeding queens solely to your local area: be prepared to travel further afield to find the perfect parents for your kitten.

• Some animal-rescue centres have litters of pure-bred kittens available for re-homing from time to time. Keep in touch with the good cat shelters in your area, but be cautious if the litter has no history (see page 69).

A CROSS-BRED OR MOGGIE KITTEN
Where to start

• Look in local newspapers for advertisements for litters that are due or for kittens already available.

• Contact the vet centres in your area. The owners of queens who have had unplanned pregnancies usually seek midwifery advice, and vet centres often try to help in finding good homes for the kittens.

• Contact cat-rescue organizations in your area. If you are a first-time cat-owner, you should really avoid kittens who are not with their mother (see page 69).

What to do next

• If possible, visit several pregnant queens to meet them and their owners. If none of the queens on your initial shortlist meets your expectations, keep looking.

• If you meet a queen with kittens already several weeks old, and you like her, the kittens and the owner, you may have to decide on a kitten sooner than you had planned (you will find more information on how to choose your kitten from a litter on pages 68–9). However, do not miss out any of the very important preparation stages detailed in the following pages.

AN OLDER KITTEN

If you would like an older kitten, you should ideally undertake the same research as if you wanted an eight-week-old kitten. However, it may be difficult or even impossible to discover an individual's personal history.

ADVANCE PLANNING

With the research done, you should have identified the place from which you will obtain your new kitten. If your kitten is thought to have been conceived but is as yet unborn, keep in touch with the queen's owner. With luck everything will go according to plan, but you could be disappointed. For example, you could be fourth on a waiting list when only three kittens of your chosen sex are born. It does happen, so try not to build up your hopes too high. In this case, you can either wait until the queen is bred from the next time, or you must go back to your research to find another queen.

Once you know that the litter has been born, that the kittens are healthy and that there are enough for all concerned, you can make arrangements to visit them in order to begin the selection process for your particular kitten (see pages 68–9). You will also be able to put the date when he will be eight weeks old in your diary, as this is when you should collect him. You will need all the time available in the interim to get ready for his arrival. If the litter is already several weeks old by the time you first meet the kittens and their mother, you will have to start your preparations as soon as possible.

Preparing your house and garden

Your house and garden will present many potential dangers to your new kitten, so, as soon as you have a firm date for collecting him, you should begin to prepare for his arrival. Like all kittens, he will be inquisitive, wily and extremely ingenious when it comes to exploring his new territory, and will test the world around him with his paws, claws and mouth.

IN THE HOUSE

You should aim to make your house as safe as possible for your kitten, but within reason and without leaving yourself an empty cell to live in!

Your kitten's playroom

First of all, choose a room in which you will be happy to let your new kitten play. This should be a place in which you can easily keep an eye on him, and, for the sake of hygiene and safety, it really ought to be somewhere other than the kitchen.

Spend time making sure that the room is as kitten-proof as possible. Put all electric flexes out of harm's way, remove any plants and fit guards to fireplaces. Place the furniture so as to prevent your kitten from lying directly against hot radiators, and remove any ornaments. Low cupboards should have firm catches.

Remember that your kitten will attempt to climb everything he can. Scaling curtains in particular is a mountaineering feat of great amusement to kittens: they rarely fall, but often need rescuing as it is usually only fun going up. Make sure that all escape routes to the outside world are sealed off. Even if your kitten will ultimately be able to go outdoors, you should not allow him out until he has completed his first course of vaccinations (see pages 120–1).

You will also need to decide where to put your kitten's litter-tray. Cats feel very vulnerable when they are going to the toilet, and most prefer their litter-trays to be off the beaten track. Your kitten's toilet area can be in any suitable location, but it should be nowhere near the place in which you intend to feed him.

Your kitten's bed

Put some pieces of man-made fleece rug (see page 52) in two or three places in your kitten's playroom, and let him decide where he would like to sleep. As soon as this becomes obvious, you can provide him with a more de luxe bed. My cat Gorbachov sleeps in a hammock attached to a radiator.

House rules

Whenever you are at home, you should supervise your kitten's access to other parts of your house: decide in advance which these will be. Your kitten will also need to learn what is acceptable behaviour. For instance, if he jumps on to a piece of furniture that you have set in the house rules as being out of bounds you will need to break his concentration and give him a warning, but without punishing him (see page 79). As he grows older, he will soon become trustworthy enough to be left unsupervised in places other than his playroom.

IN THE GARDEN

The great outdoors can be a hazardous place for all animals, but you will reduce the potential dangers to your kitten by taking the following steps.

Safety measures

If you have a pond, you should fit an escape ramp, or, if the pond is covered with mesh, check that there are no gaps. If you have a water butt, cover it over.

After your kitten's arrival, you will need to keep all garden implements locked away when they are not in use. Shut all gates, shed doors and windows, and take great care when using and storing garden chemicals.

As in the house, use your common sense with safety precautions in the garden. After all, if you intend to allow your kitten unrestricted access outdoors, he will venture beyond your garden unless you fence him in.

An outdoor run

If you decide to allow your kitten restricted access outdoors in a proper enclosure, now is the time to plan its design and construction (see pages 88–9). You could buy a ready-to-assemble enclosure, or you may opt to build one yourself. An alternative is to make your entire garden escape-proof using appropriate fencing.

Before you obtain your kitten, take a close look at your garden's safety from his point of view. The following is a checklist of some of the aspects to consider. 1 If you intend to restrict your kitten to your garden, install a tall perimeter fence crowned with inward-facing wire mesh. 2 Store all tools and chemicals in a locked shed, well away from the fence. 3 Cover over a water butt. 4 Your kitten is unlikely to be attracted by poisonous plants, but avoid those known to be especially hazardous. 5 Cover over a pond.

What you will need

A number of cat-care items will be essential in order to look after your kitten properly and, as with all your other preparations, you should select and buy these items ahead of his arrival.

The following are what I consider to be the most basic cat-care items that you will need. You will have to buy many of these, but you may be able to borrow others, or make them. Use the information given here to put together a shopping list.

A carrying basket

There will be times when you need a secure carrier in which to transport your kitten. There are many types available from which to choose, but I would recommend a plastic-coated wire basket with a top-opening lid. This type of carrier is easy to clean, and it is simple to lift a kitten or cat in and out of it. Other types of carrier may look more de luxe, but are much less practical. The great difficulty that I and my veterinary nurses experience in trying to remove some cats from such carriers, with their many 'paw holds', is all the evidence that we need.

Bedding

The best and cheapest option is a man-made fleece rug. This is comfortable, warm and very easy to clean. Other options are a foam-padded bed (most cats seem to prefer the covered types), or a bean-bag. Avoid a wicker basket, as it will be impossible to keep clean.

Litter-trays and litter

Most litter-trays are made of plastic, and come in a range of dazzling colours. You will need at least two trays. Go for large ones that are sufficiently deep to prevent your kitten from kicking his litter out over the edge, but shallow enough for him to climb into easily. A covered litter-tray will offer your kitten some privacy in an exposed location. Stock up with a supply of tray liners and a litter-tray scoop for cleaning.

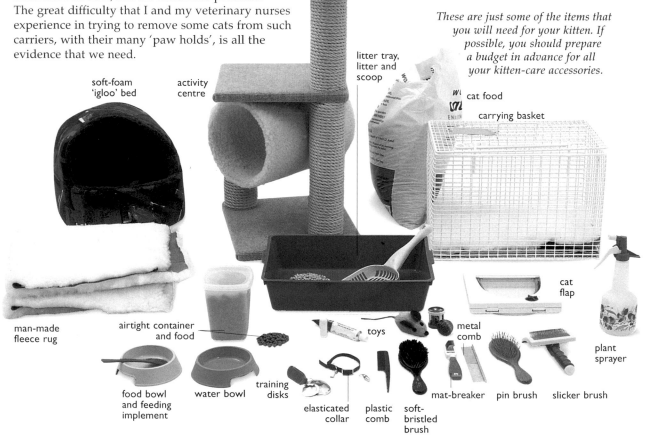

These are just some of the items that you will need for your kitten. If possible, you should prepare a budget in advance for all your kitten-care accessories.

soft-foam 'igloo' bed

activity centre

litter tray, litter and scoop

cat food

carrying basket

man-made fleece rug

airtight container and food

toys

metal comb

cat flap

plant sprayer

food bowl and feeding implement

water bowl

training disks

elasticated collar

plastic comb

soft-bristled brush

mat-breaker

pin brush

slicker brush

WHERE TO BUY CAT-CARE PRODUCTS

Many different care products are now available and – in terms of quality – you will generally get what you pay for. Only buy products that are well-packaged and properly labelled with full instructions for use. When choosing the most appropriate products for your kitten, you will be well-served by specialist outlets who employ knowledgeable staff. However, do not always assume that a large store will be the best: I have often found quite the reverse, and that the long-time owner of a small pet-accessory store may give excellent advice.

It is also now commonplace for vet centres to sell a range of specialist products (as a legal requirement, certain healthcare products are only available from vet centres). A good centre may also have trained nurses on hand as animal-care advisors. When you are making decisions that concern your kitten's health and welfare, it really does pay to talk to the experts.

For further information on using litter-trays, and on the numerous different types of cat litter available, refer to pages 74–7.

Food and feeding equipment

You should decide what you are going to feed your kitten – and how you will feed it – well in advance of collecting him (see pages 54–67). For the first day or so you will keep him on the same diet that his breeder has been offering him (see page 63), but this will then change. Buy your kitten's food near the time at which he will eat it, to ensure that it is fresh.

If you decide to offer your kitten a dry food (see page 60), you will need an airtight container in which to store it. He will also need a suitable feeding bowl and a water bowl (see page 64).

An identity collar

Depending on the cat-control laws in force where you live, you may have to obtain a collar that will carry your kitten's identification details (see page 99). You should write your name and address or telephone number directly on the collar, using indelible ink, or attach a small identity disk.

When you fit a collar to your kitten, make sure that you can easily slide two fingers (on their side) beneath it. Any collar must be designed to expand or break should an object such as a twig become caught under it when your kitten is out and about (see pages 98–9). Avoid decorating the collar with any unnecessary bells or rings that could become snagged.

Toys

Kittens have active minds as well as bodies, and your kitten's brain will need exercising as much as his body. Try to choose toys for him that will stimulate natural behaviour such as pouncing, batting and scooping (see page 85). If you wish to make some toys, you do not need to be a master craftsman, as even a screwed-up piece of paper will make a cheap and fun form of entertainment for your kitten.

Activity centres, or climbing frames (see page 84), are fairly new inventions. These are excellent, although they can be expensive. In my view, they are essential for cats who are restricted indoors.

Scratching posts

All cats are naturally driven to scratch suitable objects in their environment with their front claws, as a form of territory-marking and possibly to keep their nails in trim (see page 82). Not all cats will do this indoors: those who can go outside may do all the scratching they wish on trees and fence-posts.

An old piece of log may make a perfectly adequate scratching post indoors, or there are many purpose-built types available. Avoid buying your kitten a post that is covered in carpet, or he may simply see your wall-to-wall twist pile as a luxurious extension of it.

A cat flap

If you decide to allow your kitten outdoors when he has completed his primary-vaccination course, you will need to install a suitable cat flap (see pages 86–7).

Training equipment

Cats are perfectly trainable. To help in teaching your kitten what you consider to be unacceptable behaviour on his part, you will need a plant sprayer, or a set of training disks (see pages 78–9).

Healthcare equipment

You may already have some bathroom-style weighing scales at home; if not, you will need to buy a set. To care for your kitten's coat, you will need some specific grooming equipment (see pages 108–11). You will also need a dental-care kit (see pages 112–13) and parasite-prevention products (see pages 114–17). A first-aid kit will only be of value if you know how to use it.

Hygiene equipment

You will need special chemicals to clean up toileting accidents, and a veterinary disinfectant (see page 77).

Food and drink

The best time to make the feeding decisions that will form the basis of your kitten's future diet is before you collect him. Without him hungrily demanding his dinner, you will be much more likely to make sensible and rational choices rather than impulsive decisions.

Good nutrition

A cat's nutritional needs are very different from yours, and when it comes to his dietary requirements a kitten is a very special sort of cat. Your kitten will be what he eats: his meals will eventually turn into everything from blood cells, nerves and muscles to skin, hair and structures such as bones and teeth.

Whatever you decide to feed your kitten, that food must provide him with all the fuel that he needs, must contain the essential chemicals for his body processes to function and must supply the 'building blocks' that will allow his body to repair itself and to grow.

Formulating a balanced, nutritious diet for a kitten is a complex science, and I believe it is best left to the nutritionists employed by pet-food manufacturers. At the same time, making sure that your kitten benefits

from their skill by choosing the right products to feed him and then feeding them properly is an art, and it is on this that you should concentrate your efforts.

Over the following pages you will find important background information about food itself, on digestion and on the various prepared-food options available for cats, as well as suggestions on how to create a healthy and nutritious diet for your kitten.

WHAT IS FOOD?

Food is any solid or liquid that, when swallowed, can supply any or all of the following.
• Fuel materials that the body can use to produce movement or heat.
• The materials that are required for growth, repair or reproduction.
• The substances that are necessary to control the above body processes.

Types of nutrient

All individual food items, as well as more complex meals, are made up of varying combinations of water, plus one or more of the following five different types of food component, or nutrient.

Carbohydrates • These provide the body with fuel, and may be converted into body fat. They also affect the way in which the digestive system functions (see page 56). Examples of carbohydrates are glucose and cellulose.

Fats • Fats are the most highly concentrated source of fuel for the body. They help in the absorption of certain vitamins (see opposite, below), and provide the essential fatty acids that are required for some important body functions to take place. Fats also improve the palatability of the foods in which they are found.

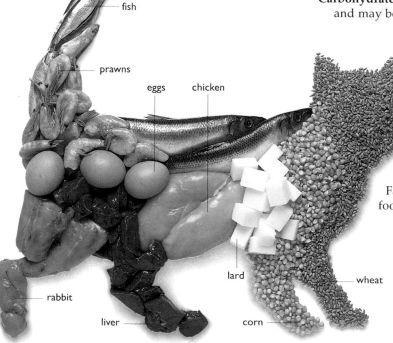

From a dietary point of view, cats are considered to be obligate carnivores and so must have foods of animal origin in their diets: they cannot survive as strict vegetarians. Shown here are some of the typical basic ingredients that may be used to make commercially prepared cat foods (see pages 58–60).

fish

prawns

eggs   chicken

lard

wheat

rabbit

liver   corn

EATING IN THE WILD

There are no scientists to help wild cats to choose a diet that will keep them fit and strong: they have to rely on a combination of instinct, their powerful senses of smell and taste, and the availability at different times of the year of the food items that comprise their diets.

Like other animals, wild cats become hungry because of their short-term need for energy, or fuel: a commodity that we measure in calories. When hunting for food, their prime concern is to fill up with fuel, but they will only stay healthy and survive in the long term if the foods that they choose not only provide them with enough calories but also contain all the other essential nutrients that their bodies require. Provided that they do not end up eating a diet that is deficient in any nutrients, they should remain healthy. Whether wild cats eat far more of some nutrients than they actually need – a situation that in pet cats we try to avoid on a long-term basis – is perhaps irrelevant to animals with a relatively short lifespan.

Pet cats, like their wild relatives, are primarily meat-eaters. They cannot survive as true vegetarians, and must have at least some meat-based food ingredients included in their diets to remain fit and healthy.

Proteins • Once they have been broken down during digestion (see page 56), proteins provide the body with substances called amino acids. These are the body's 'building blocks', essential for growth and repair. Amino acids are also used by the body to make hormones, and they can be used as fuel as and when necessary.

Minerals • These are present in foods in relatively small amounts. Minerals are involved in many of the body's most important functions, such as the way in which the nerves work. The minerals calcium and phosphorus are the main components of hard structures such as teeth and bones; other important minerals that are found in foods include sodium, magnesium and potassium.

Vitamins • Vitamins – like minerals – are present in different types of food in small amounts. The role of vitamins is to help in controlling many of the important chemical reactions and processes that take place in the body.

How does a cat process food?

The cat's digestive system is a quite remarkable food processor, in which the food that is eaten goes through a number of different stages.

The mouth • Food enters the cat's digestive system through his mouth, where it is mixed with saliva. A cat's teeth are well-suited to shearing food into small pieces, although many prepared foods (see pages 58–60) require little chewing.

The oesophagus • The swallowed food moves down this tube, which connects the mouth and stomach.

The stomach • The food is churned up here with digestive juices, which begin the breakdown of proteins. The stomach also controls a steady flow of partly digested food into the intestines.

The small intestine • This is the first and longest part of the intestines, and it is here that most digestion takes place. Fluids containing digestive enzymes are produced by the intestine and by the pancreas, a small organ best-known for making the insulin needed to control the body's sugar levels. These enzymes complete the breakdown of the proteins, carbohydrates and fats into units small enough to pass through the intestinal wall and into the body, in a process called absorption (see above, right).

The large intestine • By the time the meal reaches the large intestine, little of value remains. Bacteria digest some of the remaining protein and fibre, and, by doing so, produce substances that give a cat's faeces their characteristic smell and colour.

The rectum • Any undigested materials – together with some water, minerals and dead bacteria – are stored in this last part of the gut until the cat next goes to the toilet.

The digestive system of the cat

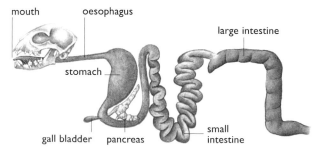

mouth   oesophagus

large intestine

stomach

gall bladder   pancreas   small intestine

The cat's digestive system is under nervous and hormonal control. It consists of a number of interconnected parts, each of which has a specific function to perform.

During the process of digestion, the wall of the small intestine contracts to help in mixing its contents. Bile is also added from the gall bladder in the liver: this contains chemicals that aid the digestion of fats.

Although some absorption goes on in the stomach and the large intestine, most of the digested nutrients (including minerals and vitamins) and water are finally taken into the body through the small intestine. Its wall is heavily folded, and covered by tiny finger-like projections that help to increase the area over which absorption can occur.

CREATING A HEALTHY DIET

The first step in feeding any cat a healthy diet is to establish the nutrients that he needs and to calculate how much of each one his body requires in order not to run out of fuel, body-building materials or other essential substances. The answer to this is called his 'nutritional need', and will depend on several factors including the cat's age and lifestyle.

Thanks to years of research by scientists employed by the best pet-food manufacturers, lists are now published that specify what are currently thought to be the minimum nutritional needs of growing kittens and adult cats. These lists are very complex and of little or no use to the majority of cat-owners, but they are extremely valuable to the people who formulate prepared foods, as well as to vets and others who advise owners on nutritional matters.

As a prospective cat-owner, you will have various options for satisfying your kitten's nutritional need, and these are outlined below and opposite.

A natural diet

If you believe that your kitten should have a totally natural diet, you could leave him to hunt for himself. However, as he will probably have had no hunting experience before he comes to live with you, and will not have been introduced to prey by his mother, he may well go hungry.

Of course, you could go out and hunt for your kitten, but how good are you likely to be at catching baby rabbits and hares? Even if you were successful, would you be prepared to show your kitten how to eat such food items?

Advantage • A very natural diet.

Disadvantages • Very messy; difficult to find the right 'ingredients'; time-consuming to prepare!

As soon as a cat starts to eat a meal, his digestive system will begin the complex process of breaking down the food into its component parts, or nutrients.

Fresh human foods

You could choose to feed your kitten solely on home-prepared fresh meat and other food items intended for human consumption, but which would you buy? You will only be able to make the correct decisions if you know precisely what nutrients each of the fresh foods contains, so that you can measure this against your kitten's nutritional need.

If you would really like to take this option, you will need some expert help and advice, as well as access to complicated data. Although it is certainly possible to feed a kitten properly in this way, I would not recommend you to do so.

Advantages • High-quality ingredients; can make a highly palatable diet.

Disadvantages • Expensive; time-consuming to prepare; waste of foods intended for humans; difficult to ensure a good nutritional balance.

Commercially prepared cat foods

You could feed your kitten entirely on commercially prepared cat foods (see pages 58–60). There is now a vast range of these products from which to choose.

Advantages • Convenient; palatable; great variety available; economical; the best prepared foods are nutritionally well-balanced; prevents wastage of foods intended for human consumption.

Disadvantages • Hard to identify good products from the less good ones; reliance on manufacturers' knowledge of cat nutrition; less owner-involvement.

Prepared and fresh foods

In my view this is the best option. By carefully selecting and using the best, and most appropriate, scientifically formulated cat foods as the major part of what you feed your kitten, you will give him all the benefits that they have to offer. It should actually be unnecessary, but supplementing these foods with very tiny amounts of a variety of other foods (see page 65) will help to compensate for any minor nutritional errors that may occur in the formulation, manufacture or use of the products. In addition, you will feel more involved on a practical level in choosing your kitten's diet.

You will be in good company: in the UK and the USA, 90 per cent of all pet-owners feed commercially prepared products (although, in my experience, few owners feed them to the exclusion of all else).

Advantages • Convenient, yet also allows owner-involvement in feeding; peace of mind for owner; palatable; economical; nutritionally sound.

Disadvantages • In my opinion, none.

The cat's digestive system is a very efficient food processor, but its powers of digestion are limited. In general, the poorer the quality of a cat's food, the more waste he will produce.

COMMERCIALLY PREPARED CAT FOODS

Given the vast range of commercially prepared pet foods now available from supermarkets, pet-accessory stores and vet centres, it is hard to believe that, in the UK, the pet-food industry is only just over 60 years old. During those years it has developed into a multi-million-pound business, with new products being launched all the time.

Some cat-owners seem rather suspicious of the nutritional quality of commercially prepared foods, but in my experience such apprehensions are fuelled through fear of the unknown. There is no doubt in my mind that the continued development of scientifically formulated and properly tested cat foods has played a considerable part in improving the overall health of the cat population over the decades.

However, some prepared cat foods are much more scientifically advanced than others, so how should you go about selecting the right product or products for your kitten? It is best to start with the basics.

PET-FOOD INGREDIENTS

Over 98 per cent of prepared pet foods sold in the UK are made by members of the Pet Food Manufacturers' Association. As members, they agree to use in their foods only materials from those animals passed as fit for human consumption (these materials are often the parts that we would not normally eat, such as lung).

The manufacturers also agree to use nothing from horses, ponies, whales, seals or kangaroos, and they only use tuna caught in a way that does not endanger dolphins. A company that makes this agreement is not, however, legally bound by it.

The choice of prepared cat foods now available from a range of different outlets – including supermarkets, pet-accessory stores and vet centres – is enormous. You will therefore benefit from some impartial expert advice in selecting the foods that are most appropriate for your kitten.

Commercially prepared cat foods are food items intended for feline consumption that have been formulated and processed by a commercial company. From now on, I will refer to these types of foods simply as prepared cat foods.

From the nutritional point of view, there are only two types of prepared cat food available, as described below.

Complete foods

Complete cat foods must contain at least the minimum recommended amounts of each of the nutrients required by the type of cat for whom the products are intended. Made from mixtures of several ingredients, they are designed to be used as all-in-one diets without the need for any supplementation with other foods, although minor additions of certain food items (see page 65) should not adversely affect the overall balance of a cat's diet. Some complete foods are sold as suitable for cats of all ages and lifestyles, while others are intended to satisfy more specific needs, such as those of growing kittens.

Advantages • Convenient; major nutritional decisions should be taken by manufacturer and not left to owner; should be easy to use, although the labelling can be confusing (see pages 61–2).

Disadvantage • Reliance on nutritional knowledge of the manufacturer; an important consideration, as a particular food could be the sole food eaten by a cat for his entire life from weaning. Even very minor errors in the nutritional balance of a complete food could then be of more major significance in the long term.

Complementary foods

These foods are not intended to be fed as a cat's entire diet, but just as a part of it. They may be made from just one ingredient, or from a number of ingredients

FOOD TESTING

If a food claims to be complete, it is important to know how that claim is justified. After all, that food may be fed as a cat's sole source of nutrients for a number of years, so any small mistakes in its formulation could possibly affect his long-term health. The best foods will have been tested by both of the methods described below, although most manufacturers do not state their testing procedures on product labels. To obtain further information, you will therefore need to write to the manufacturer concerned.

LABORATORY ANALYSIS
The first, and simplest, method is for a manufacturer to analyse a product in a laboratory in order to find out what the food contains. Provided that it has enough of the correct nutrients to match the published minimum nutritional requirements for a cat of the sort for whom the food is intended, it may be called complete. However, this type of test only checks the quantities of the nutrients in a food, and not their quality.

FEEDING TRIALS
These tests are used to measure a product's overall quality. The food that is under test is fed to a group of appropriate cats, and scientists then measure how the cats get on and how well they digest the food.

mixed together. Single-ingredient 'gourmet-style' foods are examples of complementary foods.

Advantage • The use of complementary foods allows greater owner-involvement in feeding.

Disadvantages • Owners have to make important nutritional decisions as to which foods to combine and in what quantities in order to create a well-balanced diet; easy to overfeed.

FORMS OF PREPARED CAT FOOD

Complete and complementary cat foods are available in three different forms, depending on the amount of water that they contain. Cat-food products may be sold comprising foods in more than one form: for example, with both dry and semi-moist components. Provided that a cat is quite happy to eat enough of a particular food or foods to provide himself with all the nutrients that he needs, it does not matter to him what form those foods are in.

The different forms of cat food each have a number of potential advantages and disadvantages.

Dry foods

The majority of dry cat foods contain between 5 and 12 per cent water. Generally produced as 'nuggets' in different shapes and sizes, complete dry foods are made from a variety of plant and animal ingredients (these must be dry before being processed, so fresh animal tissues cannot be used in their formulation). The ingredients are steamed at high temperatures and are then cut into a range of shapes. These pieces are dried and finally sprayed with fat.

Advantages • Economical, as can be bought in bulk and as relatively small amounts – compared with foods containing more water – are required to provide all the nutrients a cat needs (the cost of feeding a dry food may be as little as one-third of that of feeding a semi-moist or moist food of the same nutritional quality); left out in the air, dry foods do not spoil as quickly as foods containing more water, so they can be fed on a 'self-service' basis; may help to control periodontal disease (see pages 112–13); very easy and clean to use; usually only a slight odour is detectable by humans at a distance; easy to store.

Disadvantages • Perceived as 'boring' and also 'unnatural' by many owners (in most cases their cats tend to disagree); generally less digestible and less palatable than moist foods; shorter shelf-life than other food forms.

Semi-moist foods

Most of these foods contain between 15 and 50 per cent water. The semi-moist foods with the lowest water content may be similar in appearance to dry foods, whereas those containing the most water may look and feel like minced or cubed meat.

Portions are normally sealed in foil sachets, and several sachets are then packed together in a box. Semi-moist foods are made from a mixture of meats

Prepared cat foods are available in the above three forms. None is nutritionally 'better' than the others; each has some practical advantages and disadvantages.

and cereals, formed into a paste that is moulded into shape before being cut into small pieces.

Advantages • These foods usually have only a mild odour; can be left out longer than moist foods, so suitable for feeding on a 'self-service' basis.

Disadvantages • There is little choice, as relatively few products are available in this form; generally more expensive to feed than equivalent dry foods.

Moist foods

Moist foods usually contain between 60 and 85 per cent water, and the majority are cooked. Most are made by putting the mixed ingredients into cans or trays sealed with suitable lids; these are then pressure-cooked. Typical ingredients in many complete moist foods are different kinds of meat (including fish), vegetables and cereals.

Advantages • Generally more palatable and digestible than other food forms; a wide choice of products is available; long shelf-life (particularly in the case of canned foods).

Disadvantages • More expensive to feed than an equivalent dry food; more messy to use; foods dry out quickly if left in the air, so are unsuitable for feeding on a 'self-service' basis.

USING PREPARED CAT FOODS

There is a great deal of useful information to be found on the labels of prepared cat foods. This will not only help you to choose the most suitable products for your kitten, but also to feed them properly.

It is impossible to use prepared cat foods correctly without understanding this label information. You may have to search for it, however, as a considerable amount of the space available on many labels is taken up by advertising and marketing paraphernalia. Many manufacturers seem to believe – perhaps with good reason – that cat-owners lack sufficient interest and knowledge to read important nutritional information about their foods. It is up to us to prove them wrong.

Fortunately, there are laws that dictate what must be stated on cat-food labels. In the UK (this may vary from country to country, depending on national laws relating to cat-food labelling) there are currently eight important questions about a prepared cat food to which you should be able to find answers.

Who is the food intended for?

The label must say what kind of animal the food is intended for. If it simply states that it is a food for cats, it must be suitable for cats of all ages, from weaning to very old age. Some products are intended for specific types of cat – such as growing kittens – but the best manufacturers will define what they mean by kittens (for example, they may state that the food is for kittens of up to 12 months old).

Do not choose a prepared food for your kitten that is intended for dogs. Cats have some very specific nutritional requirements, and may become seriously ill if fed with certain dog foods on a long-term basis.

What type of food is it?

Is it a complete or a complementary food? You must find this out, as it will affect all your other feeding decisions. Remember that a complete food does not need any supplementation; a complementary food does (see pages 58–9).

What is the food made from?

The list of ingredients may not be as informative as you might think. Manufacturers have the legal choice of listing every ingredient or of giving group names such as 'meat and animal derivatives', 'cereals' or 'derivatives of vegetable origin'. Group names tend to be the norm, especially on those labels that have only limited space. The ingredients list is written in decreasing order by weight.

How much of each nutrient is there?

The typical analysis lists the protein, oil (fat) and ash (effectively the total quantity of minerals in the food). The amounts of each nutrient will be given either as a percentage by weight, or per 100 g (4 oz) of the food. The analysis will also tell you how much fibre the food contains, and may indicate the water content (this will be given as a percentage figure).

Depending on the law of a particular country, only certain vitamins need to be listed on a pet-food label, and then only if they have been added separately to the recipe. The amount of carbohydrate contained in the food is unlikely to be specified, but can be calculated from the other figures given.

Cats of different ages have different nutritional needs. This young kitten and adult cat will benefit from eating foods that have been specifically formulated and scientifically proven to meet their individual requirements.

If you decide to feed a dry food to your kitten you will need an airtight container in which to store it, so as to preserve its nutritional quality and freshness.

Does the food contain additives?

Extra vitamins, flavours, preservatives and colouring agents are all examples of additives that may be used in certain cat foods. Additives as a whole tend to have a bad reputation, but many are essential in ensuring that the products are safe and nutritious to eat. Most additives used in pet foods are also found in human foods, and are only added in the smallest amounts necessary. When any preservatives or colouring agents have been used it should say so on the label, although specific chemical names are unlikely to be given.

Is the food fresh?

A 'best-before' date should be somewhere on the container (this may not be on the label itself).

Who makes the food?

If you would like more information about a particular food, such as the ways in which it has been tested (see page 59), you will need to contact the company responsible for making the food: an address should be supplied on the label.

How should the food be used?

You will find feeding instructions on the label. Every cat is an individual – even two cats of the same breed and size may need different amounts of food to stay healthy – so it is impossible for a manufacturer to give precise feeding instructions that will suit all the cats for whom a product is intended. Instead, suggestions should be offered in the form of a feeding guide.

Unfortunately, such guides often tend to be rather unclear and are sometimes misleading. If you consider a feeding guide on a product to be confusing, choose another product. I have no doubt that the only way in which such feeding guides will improve is if owners vote with their purses. If it is a complementary food (see page 59), the label should tell you what else you need to feed to create a balanced diet for your kitten.

On a well-labelled food, the feeding guide should be self-explanatory, but remember that the suggested daily feeding amount is only a starting point. You will need to adjust the quantity that you offer your kitten depending on his weight and condition (see page 65). Take note of any special advice that is offered about the preparation or use of the food.

SELECTING A PREPARED FOOD

The final decision as to which product or products you use will be a very personal one. If the kitten you are about to obtain will be the first cat you have ever looked after, obtaining some expert advice will save you a lot of time and effort, and a great deal of worry.

Asking the experts

If you do seek advice, make sure that it comes from someone knowledgeable about cat nutrition. Every person who has ever fed a cat will probably offer you an opinion on how to feed your kitten. Some of this – especially practical hints and tips on feeding – will be useful, but beware of the views of self-proclaimed nutrition 'experts' who have no scientific training.

One option is to ask your vet or a veterinary nurse who is interested in nutrition what he or she would use to feed a kitten of the type that you plan to have. If you would like to be more involved in making the final decision yourself, why not ask for a shortlist of several suitable products, from which you can make a final selection? If you have the time available, you could also ask a number of experienced owners for recommendations, and then assess each one in detail before speaking to an expert advisor.

Tips on choosing a prepared food

The advice that I offer my clients is as follows.
• Aim to select just one brand of complete food at first. This brand – or varieties of it – should account for at least 90 per cent of what your kitten eats.
• Choose a food specifically formulated for growing kittens, and avoid those foods claiming to be suitable for any cat of any age.
• Choose a food that is made by a reputable company, and find out how the food has been tested. Only select a food that has been tested by laboratory analysis and feeding trials (see page 59).

• When comparing the relative costs of the different foods, do not look just at the product prices but work out how much of each food your kitten will need to eat each day and then calculate the cost. In general, a cat will need to eat less of a more expensive food than he would require of a cheaper one to stay healthy.

• Spend as much as you can afford on your kitten's food products. Cheap foods tend to contain cheap ingredients, whereas more expensive foods are usually made from better-quality ingredients, by companies that have invested in scientific research.

• Choose products that are very clearly labelled with comprehensive feeding instructions. Always follow these instructions carefully.

• Remember that you can always change your mind at a later date. However good the food that you have chosen may be, it will have no nutritional value at all to your kitten if he dislikes it for some reason and it remains uneaten in his bowl.

FEEDING YOUR KITTEN

When you bring your kitten home, you will be able to put all the theory into practice. When you collect him, make sure that you find out from his breeder what he has been fed on since weaning, and ask if you can buy a small amount of that food to give him for the first few days when he comes home with you.

Professional breeders tend to have very strong views about how to feed kittens. Some are very knowledgeable and up-to-date while others have more traditional views, but do not let either sort change the decisions you have made. Provided that you have been sensible about making

The amount that a kitten needs to eat depends on his personal requirements and the nutritional quality of his food. Each of the bowls below contains a daily portion of a complete food suitable for this 12-month-old moggie kitten.

your choices, and you have also obtained appropriate expert advice, be prepared to stick by them.

On day one, feed your kitten the diet to which he is accustomed and then, on day two, begin to mix in some of the new food that you have chosen. He may turn up his nose at the new food initially. If it is a dry food, leave some out for your kitten to come back to whenever he wishes (see below), or, if you are offering a moist food, warm it a little. Be patient. If your kitten continues to refuse his food, contact your vet centre for advice. If all goes well, he should be completely on to his new food by the end of the first week.

How many meals a day?

Young kittens have small stomachs, and need their total daily food allocation split into a number of small meals in order to prevent their digestive systems from becoming overloaded. Even as adults, some cats seem to prefer to eat 10 or more meals each day. If you are feeding a dry food to your kitten (see page 60), you should be able to offer it to him on a 'self-service' basis without getting into problems, but you must weigh him regularly to make sure that he does not put on too much weight. If he does so, you will have to restrict him to a number of set meals. Do not leave moist foods out for more than about 20 minutes, or they will become dry and unpalatable.

How much to feed?

The total amount of food that your kitten needs each day will depend not only on the type of food that you give him, but also on his age, weight, activity level and the rate at which his body burns up calories even when he is asleep. Every kitten is different, and two kittens of the same age, sex, weight and breed are likely to need slightly different amounts of the same food to stay healthy and to grow properly (see also page 65).

reasonable-quality dry food

higher-quality dry food

reasonable-quality moist food

higher-quality moist food

Where to feed?

This is up to you, but I would recommend somewhere away from the normal hustle and bustle of family life, where your kitten can eat in peace and quiet.

If you have an older cat, he will be on a different diet. One good way of preventing an adult cat from eating a kitten's food is to place the youngster's food inside an upturned box with a small hole cut in it. As he grows, you can simply increase the size of the hole.

Who should do the feeding?

Your kitten will respect the hand that feeds him, so ideally this is a job in which all the members of the family should take a part.

Every member of the family should be involved in feeding your kitten. Cats trust those who feed them, and feeding time is a good opportunity to strengthen the bonds between your kitten and those who live with him.

What to feed in?

You should buy your kitten's food bowl in advance. In my experience, the best types are made of stainless steel or plastic, and are wider at the base than they are at the top. A bowl of this kind will be easy to keep clean, indestructible and stable.

Choose a bowl with a non-slip base so that your kitten cannot turn it into an ice-hockey puck. It should also be shallow and fairly wide so that he will not keep brushing his whiskers on the edge while he is eating. Avoid a bowl that is designed to contain both food and water, or the water will end up as soup.

What about variety?

Many cats seem to be very happy to eat the same type of food every day for long periods. It will be much better – especially at first – to concentrate on feeding one high-quality complete food to your kitten than to try to mix and match a number of different foods while still maintaining an overall nutritional balance.

However, if after some time your kitten begins to refuse a food that he has been perfectly happy to eat for some time, it may be that he is a cat who would benefit from a little variety in his diet. Some specific brands of food may be available in different varieties and so – provided that all the varieties are equivalent from a nutritional point of view – you should be able to solve the problem without having to search for alternative brands.

Taste versus quality

Try to avoid getting into the habit of selecting foods simply because your kitten finds them tasty. The foods that he considers the most palatable may not be the best for him from a nutritional point of view, so do not allow taste to become the sole deciding factor.

Fussy eaters

A word of warning. Offering your kitten too much variety in his food can cause problems, as he may continually accept and then reject new foods if you keep responding to what you believe is his dislike of a new food by offering something else. You will then run out of good-quality foods to offer and, like many owners in this situation, you will probably resort to highly palatable, unbalanced foods in order to keep your kitten happy. A big mistake!

What about other foods?

As has already been discussed, complete kitten foods are designed to be fed on their own, with no other foods added (see pages 58–9). However, I would not discourage you from adding to your kitten's diet very small amounts of other food items if you wish (see page 57 and below).

Provided that you choose any other food items with care, and that as a whole they account for less than 10 per cent of the total amount of food that your kitten consumes each day, they should not adversely affect the balance of his overall diet. Try to avoid adding fatty foods that are high in calories.

The following is a list of the items that you may consider adding to your kitten's diet.

Fresh meat • This should be fit for you to eat, and cooked. It is low in minerals and vitamins.

Fish • Fish is a good source of protein, but is low in important minerals and vitamins. Any bones should be removed to prevent choking. Always cook fish before feeding it to your kitten.

Eggs • If possible, feed egg yolk and white together. If fed on its own, egg white should be cooked as, when raw, it contains a substance that can destroy an important B vitamin.

Cheese • This is a good source of protein and fat, but watch the extra calories.

Liver • Liver is most nutritious if fed raw, but may cause diarrhoea. If fed in excessive amounts, liver can cause serious illness.

Table scraps • Avoid giving your kitten sauces and other human food dressings, as many of these may upset his digestion.

What about special supplements?

You may be tempted to add some of the items listed overleaf to your kitten's diet. However, each of these items has potential drawbacks and could even be harmful to your kitten.

CHECKING ON PROGRESS

When calculating how much of a particular food your kitten should eat, the only sensible way to start is to weigh your kitten and then to follow the feeding guide on the product label (see page 62). If your kitten's age or weight lies between the weight examples given, make a sensible estimate. Be sure to measure out all your kitten's food portions accurately.

YOUR KITTEN'S WEIGHT

By regularly weighing your kitten and comparing his weight with a feeding guide and a typical growth curve (see page 36), you will be able to adjust the amount of food that you give him as he grows. Few kittens will eat more than they actually need, so you should be able to feed your kitten on demand, or on a 'self-service' basis.

Note: for reasons of hygiene, if you use a set of ordinary kitchen scales – such as those shown here – to weigh your kitten, you must make absolutely sure that the dish is not used subsequently for weighing or preparing food for human consumption.

HEALTH-CHECKS
Your vet or veterinary nurse will monitor your kitten's growth and development at his regular health-checks (see page 66). At these appointments, the vet or nurse will be able to help you with any feeding queries that you may have.

Fats and oils • Some owners believe that adding fats and oils to their cats' diets will improve the condition of their coats, but a cat who is fed on a high-quality complete food does not need them. Indeed, offering extra calories to your kitten in this highly concentrated form will not only reduce the amount of the prepared food that he needs to eat, but even small amounts could also seriously upset the overall nutritional balance of his diet.

Vitamins and minerals • These are essential if a home-made diet is being fed (see page 57), but are totally unnecessary and may even be harmful if a good-quality prepared food is being used.

Herbal and plant supplements • Few – if any – health benefits have been scientifically proven from the use of these supplements. This is not to say that they do not work, but you should exercise great caution when offering such supplements to your kitten, because some of the most powerful drugs are plant extracts. Many herbs and other plants can also be poisonous to cats if they are fed in the wrong amounts.

Chocolate • This contains a substance that is actually poisonous to cats. Unsweetened baking chocolate is the most dangerous type.

Development checks

Many first-time kitten-owners worry endlessly about whether they have made the right feeding choices for their kittens. The most important test of the feeding regime that you have adopted is to take a close look at your kitten and at the waste he produces (see above, right), and this is one of the reasons why health-checks at your vet centre are so important.

Ideally, once a month you should take your kitten to see his vet or veterinary nurse, who will make sure that he is healthy and in good condition. By weighing him, he or she can create a personal growth chart for comparison with normal charts for kittens of his type (see page 36), to ensure that he is not growing too fast or too slowly and that he is not overweight.

WARNING

If you decide to change your kitten's diet, you should make any changes slowly by mixing some of his old and new food together for a few days. Making any sudden changes – even between two good-quality foods – is likely to cause a bout of diarrhoea.

The amount of water that a cat obtains from his food will depend on its form. A typical can of moist prepared food for cats contains up to 85 per cent water – the amount shown in these beakers.

At home, you must check your kitten's faeces. If his droppings are very loose, you may be giving him too much at each meal. Large volumes of bulky faeces are often produced by kittens fed on poorer-quality foods.

Moving on to adult food

If, as I have recommended (see page 57), you choose to feed your kitten a complete food specifically made for kittens, you should change him on to a complete food for adult cats at or near the time he stops gaining weight. This will be when he is about one year old (check this on the feeding guide of his current food).

WATER

A cat can survive for weeks without food, but will only remain alive for a few days at the most without water. The average adult cat contains 3 litres (5 pints) of water, accounting for 60 per cent of his body weight.

Water enables all of the body's essential chemical reactions to take place, and is the main component of blood. It is very involved in body-temperature control, and is needed for the digestive system to function.

Inputs and outputs

Like all cats, your kitten will be constantly losing water from his body in his faeces and urine, in the air that he breathes out, in the small amount of sweat he produces through his feet and nose, and in his other body secretions. All this water must be replenished.

Some of what your kitten needs will be produced by his body as it burns up food to produce energy, but most will either come as part of his food or through drinking fresh water.

A typical complete dry food contains only 5 to 12 per cent water. A cat fed on food in this form will therefore need to drink considerably more water each day than a cat fed on a nutritionally equivalent moist food.

How much water does a cat need?

An average adult cat will require a minimum of about 150 ml (¼ pt) of water per day, and he will obtain this from his food and from drinking.

The amount that your kitten drinks will depend on how much water he takes in with his food. Remember that a can of moist prepared cat food may contain up to 85 per cent water, whereas a dry food may contain only 5 per cent. As it is impossible to know exactly how much water your kitten will lose each day, you should make sure that he always has access to fresh water. He can then adjust his intake to suit himself.

OTHER DRINKS

Fresh, clean tap water is the only drink that your kitten should need.

What about milk?

Many owners feel that they should give their kittens milk to drink as well as water. Milk is very nutritious, but if you are feeding your kitten on a balanced, good-quality food he will not need it. In addition, his ability to digest lactose – one of the sugars in milk – will have declined at weaning (see page 32), so he could suffer from diarrhoea if you offer it to him.

Lactose-reduced drinks

If you decide to offer your kitten such a product, remember that its contents may affect the overall nutritional balance of his diet.

Water plays a vital role in keeping a cat healthy. The quantity of water that your kitten needs each day will depend on various factors, including his body weight. This older kitten's daily water requirement from all sources will be about 200 ml (⅓ pint).

Choosing your kitten

When picking out a young kitten from a litter, remember that there is no single 'best' kitten: each one will have his own good points and bad points. If possible, you should visit the litter several times before you make your final selection, as you will then gain a much better impression of the characters of the individual kittens.

Choosing the right kitten is an important decision, so plan your visits to the breeder carefully. Each time you visit, observe the kittens from a distance before interacting with them. It is very tempting just to dive into the middle of the litter to play with them, but try to avoid acting on impulse. Instead, follow the step-by-step guide given here, and you will be much more likely to end up with the right kitten for your family.

1 Make your final visit to the litter when the kittens are six to eight weeks old. If your kitten is old enough to go home with you the same day (at eight weeks), try to make the visit on a day when you will be at home for at least the next two days to look after him: a weekend is ideal. You should be completely prepared for your kitten at home (see pages 50–1). You should also have a suitable carrier for him (see page 52), and your vet should be expecting to see you later in the day (see pages 70–1).

If possible, all those who will live with your kitten should go with you, but any children must understand the importance of the choice that you are about to make, and what to do when you all get there. Make it clear, too, that you will have the final decision.

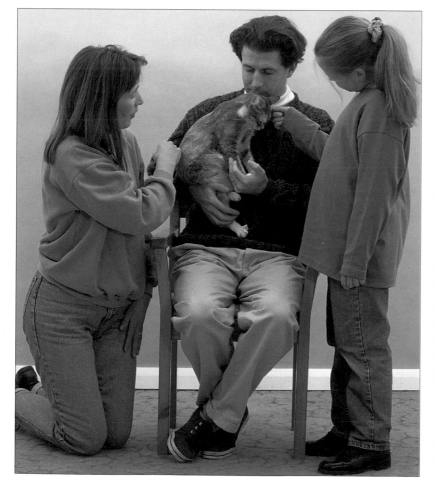

2 When you first arrive at the breeder's house, spend several minutes watching the litter playing together, and interacting with the queen and the breeder.

Try to form an opinion as to the temperament of each of the kittens. Some kittens are obviously quieter than others, some are definitely shy and others are full of their own self-confidence. Ask the breeder what he or she thinks of each of the kittens, having seen them every day.

3 Ask to have a closer look just at the kittens of the right sex who are still available. You should have spent some time getting to know the kittens' mother on previous visits, so she and the rest of the litter can be taken away so that they will not be a distraction. With the remaining shortlisted kittens, do not actively play with them at first, but just sit on the floor and

On your first visit to see a breeder or a litter, spend time with the queen to be bred from (or the kittens' mother). If in any way she is not the type of cat you would like to own, go no further.

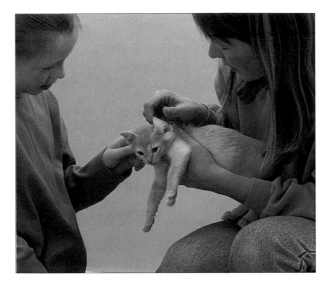

Carry out a simple health-check on your favourite kitten (see pages 106–7). This should enable you to identify any obvious problems, and to see how tolerant he is of being handled.

see how they interact with you. Once the kittens have become used to you, play with them a little.

Having spent some time with all the kittens, take a closer look at them individually. Carry out a simple health-check on each kitten (see pages 106–7) and, if you are in doubt about anything, ask the breeder.

4 Making the final decision is never easy. You will probably want to take all the kittens home, but stick to your decision about numbers and about the sex of your kitten or kittens (see pages 46–7).

Once you have made your choice, let the breeder know, but explain that this is subject to the approval of your vet. Make sure that, when you leave with your kitten, you have all the following items.
• A receipt for the money that you have paid.
• Your kitten's pedigree-registration papers (if any).
• Insurance documents (if any).
• Your kitten's vaccination record (if any).
• His worming record, including the timing of any procedures carried out and the products used.
• His medical record, including the details of any treatments carried out by the breeder or a vet.
• Feeding notes, to include details of current foods being offered, and timings and sizes of meals. If possible, take away with you some of your kitten's current food items so that you can slowly change him over to the food that you have chosen (see page 63).

• Details of the type of cat litter that your kitten is accustomed to using.
• A piece of your kitten's bedding, so that he will have something that smells familiar in his new home.

Choosing a kitten from a rescue centre

If you are an inexperienced cat-owner, and you are interested in a young kitten at a rescue centre but his mother is not available for you to see, be sure to seek some expert advice before making a final decision to take on the kitten (see below).

Choosing an older kitten

Spend time with any older kitten in whom you are interested, handling him and playing with him to see how he responds to you. A kitten who has had little experience of people will be shy in your company, and will be anxious and possibly aggressive if handled.

If you would like a second opinion, ask a veterinary nurse or animal-behaviour expert to look at the kitten.

Your kitten at home

With all the important preparations made well in advance, the real fun can begin. However, there is still work to do: you will need to settle your kitten into his new surroundings, teach him the rules of the house, introduce him to any other pets with whom he will live, and generally help him to adapt to his new lifestyle.

Collecting your kitten

The day on which you collect your new kitten will be an exciting and potentially stressful one for all of you. When you arrive home, you must remember that your house – and the people and other animals who live there – will be an alien environment to the kitten, so it will take him time to settle in. Do not rush him: it is very important that he has the peace and quiet to explore his new home at his own pace.

You should transport your kitten in a proper carrying basket or box. A strong plastic-coated wire basket is ideal, but a flat-packed corrugated plastic or tough cardboard carrier will do.

TRAVELLING HOME

Your kitten should travel in a suitable and strong pet carrier with a piece of man-made fleece rug inside it (see page 52). Place a folded newspaper underneath the fleece to absorb any urine.

Where to put your kitten

If you are travelling by car, the carrier must be secure. Either place it in one of the footwells – your kitten will then be well-protected should you have to brake suddenly – or secure it on a back seat using a seatbelt. If you have an estate car, you could put the basket in the back, but make sure that it cannot slide about.

Driving safely

Remember that this is likely to be your kitten's first trip in a moving vehicle, so take it steadily. Avoid fast cornering, as well as sudden braking or accelerating.

If your kitten seems anxious when travelling in his basket, cover it over with a towel to make him feel more secure. Do not open the basket in order to stroke him: you will not reassure him, and you will give him an opportunity to escape. A kitten – or an adult cat – loose in a car is a serious safety hazard.

AT YOUR VET CENTRE

If your kitten is unvaccinated, keep him in the car until your appointment, as you will not know what animals have been in the waiting room that day, or from what they were suffering. The waiting room should be well-disinfected, but it is sensible to be cautious. If it is not possible to wait in your car, sit away from any other cats and keep your kitten's basket on your lap.

Your vet will give your kitten a full examination to make sure that he is fit and well, and is not suffering from any obvious developmental problems. If your vet does discover a problem, he or she will help you to decide what action to take.

Your vet should weigh your kitten and enter his weight on a new medical record. He or she will also ask to see the papers that you obtained from his breeder, to check on previous medical treatments. Depending on your kitten's age your vet may give him a vaccine (see pages 120–1), and may also administer a worming dose (see pages 114–16). If you have decided to have your kitten identified with a microchip (see page 99), this may be carried out then and there.

Final queries

Now is the time to ask questions on any issues about which you are uncertain: your vet or a veterinary nurse should be happy to run through with you again any matters that you may have discussed together when planning for your kitten's arrival. Before you leave the vet centre, make sure that you know when

At your kitten's initial veterinary check, your vet will give him a very thorough examination to make sure that he is healthy and is not suffering from any obvious anatomical abnormalities or other disorders.

HANDLING A KITTEN

Whenever you interact with your kitten, it is important that he knows where you are and what is happening. Can you imagine how it must feel to be unexpectedly grabbed from behind? Get down to your kitten's level so that you will be less intimidating to him.

To pick up your kitten, cup one hand under his chest, and use the other to support his rear end (if he is a wriggler, you may need to place both hands around his chest). Lift him off the ground and bring him close to your body, holding him firmly but not too tightly. When you put your kitten down, place him on the ground: do not let him jump out of your arms.

As your kitten grows, you may need to adapt the way in which you pick him up. Unless you have very large hands, use both hands to hold him around his chest before gathering up his rear end under one arm (if you try this with just one hand, he is likely to jump away from you as soon as he is off the ground).

Do not carry your kitten outside unless he already has access outdoors as, if he is startled by something, he may escape from your arms and disappear.

---

and how to worm your kitten (see pages 114–16), when he will need further vaccinations and when he should return for his next development check.

FITTING YOUR KITTEN'S COLLAR

If you have decided to use a collar to identify your kitten (see pages 98–9), you should fit it as soon as possible. Place it around your kitten's neck, and fasten it so that you can easily slip two fingers underneath without pulling the collar tight.

Your kitten will almost certainly scratch at the collar for a while as he will find it rather a strange sensation around his neck at first, but he is unlikely to remove it. And with so many other things to think about at the moment, it should not worry him for long.

TALKING TO YOUR KITTEN

As soon as you have collected your kitten, start talking to him. He will need to become accustomed to your normal voice, so try not to speak to him in 'baby talk'.

Every time you say anything to your kitten, use his new name: the sooner he recognizes it, the easier it will be for you to gain his attention in the future.

Arriving home

As soon as you reach home, quickly finish off the preparations in your kitten's playroom. Fill his litter-tray with the litter that he is accustomed to using, and, if he has been fed 'ad-lib' on a dry food by his breeder, fill up his bowl. Place the piece of bedding from his former home near his bowl, as the smell of the food and bedding will make him feel at home.

Once your kitten is confident in his new surroundings, you should all handle him frequently in order to accustom him to you and to gain his trust.

Make sure that all doors and windows are shut, then bring in your kitten. Carefully turn the basket on its side and open the lid, then stand back and let the kitten venture out into the room at his own speed. Talk to him quietly, but avoid trying to pick him up. Once you are happy that he has found his food bowl, litter-tray and old piece of bedding, leave the room. Come back regularly and frequently in order to keep an eye on him, but try not to disturb him too much.

Family introductions

Although all the members of your family will have greeted your new kitten, he will not yet have had the chance to get to know and trust them. Rather than all piling into his playroom together, go to see him in turns at first. Make sure that everyone behaves in the same quiet way: no-one should seize the kitten for a cuddle unless he initiates such interaction. Any care activities such as emptying his litter-tray or feeding him should be done quietly. Leave a piece of dirty clothing belonging to each member of your family with your kitten. By sniffing at this clothing, he will be able to familiarize himself with all your personal scents.

Your kitten and children

It is essential that your kitten learns to trust any children you may have. The children must remain quiet and calm when they are with him, and young children should be supervised. They should understand that a friendly kitten is not as demonstrative as a puppy, and that he may not come bounding over to greet them.

As soon as possible, sensible older children should be encouraged to handle your kitten and to be involved in his care. In my experience, some older children make more diligent pet-owners than their parents! By feeding your kitten his normal food at mealtimes and hand-feeding him tiny amounts of the same food at other times, the younger members of your kitten's new family should soon gain his trust.

Beyond the playroom

Once your kitten is familiar with his playroom, and before you introduce him to any other pets that you may have, allow him to explore other areas in your house to which you have decided he will be

Your kitten's introduction to another pet should be carefully supervised. You must be in control at all times to ensure that neither animal becomes stressed or inadvertently injured.

You will find it easier to supervise this first meeting if you know what to expect. Provided that the territory is familiar, two cats meeting for the first time are likely to ignore their surroundings and concentrate on each other. Their initial investigations will probably be nose-to-nose. Depending on your kitten's personality, he may become frightened or confused, and may arch his back with his coat on end in an attempt to show some bravado; he may even hiss (see pages 38–40).

Your older cat may simply ignore your kitten, or he may try to sniff down his neck and then along his side towards his anal region. At any stage, one or the other may become threatening, but if all goes well they will quickly grow bored of each other. After the meeting, separate the cats and repeat the process at another time and in another place. Do not allow them unsupervised access to each other until you are confident that fur will not fly as soon as your back is turned.

Introducing a dog

A dog could cause great physical and mental damage to your kitten simply by wanting to play with him. Equally, your kitten could inflict nasty wounds on your dog's face with his claws. Let them experience each other's scents before they meet (see left).

When you introduce them for the first time, keep the kitten in his basket and your dog on a lead. If the kitten has been used to a dog since he was born, he may be fearless, and a dog who is used to cats should be the same; other dogs may be very excitable at first.

Only allow your kitten and dog access to each other when they are happy in each other's company. Take your kitten out of his basket and let him investigate the dog, who should be on a lead (the dog may have been calm in your kitten's presence until now, but may chase him if the kitten makes any sudden movements). Even when you can trust them together unsupervised, always provide your kitten with an escape route.

allowed supervised access. Let him investigate one room at a time, and make sure that he can always bolt back to the safety of his playroom should he be startled by something. This gradual acclimatization may take several days.

Introducing a cat

The introduction between your kitten and a resident cat should be taken very slowly. Make sure that the older cat's vaccinations are up-to-date before he meets your kitten, and allow each to become familiar with the smell of the other by swapping over a small piece of their bedding for a few days. Alternatively, rub each cat with a clean towel, and then leave this with the other to investigate.

When they first meet, your kitten and cat should be on territory that is familiar to both. Give your kitten an escape route such as an upturned cardboard box with a small hole cut in it (make sure that he is aware of this, and knows how to use it).

Ideally, have someone else with you to supervise the meeting, then let the animals get on with it. Only become involved if they start threatening each other: a broom to keep them apart and a towel to throw may be handy. If your kitten and cat do try to fight, do not put them together again until you have sought advice from your vet or from an animal-behaviour expert.

SOLVING PROBLEMS

Remember that there is no one correct way to settle a kitten into his new home. Your kitten will not have read this book, and he may not behave exactly as I have suggested. If you do experience difficulties in settling your kitten at home, or in introducing him to other animals or people, do not struggle on without help. Ask for advice at your vet centre, as your vet or a veterinary nurse may be able to provide a solution or put you in touch with an animal-behaviour expert.

Toileting

Fortunately, pet cats are naturally very clean animals when it comes to their toileting habits. From just a few weeks of age a kitten has control of his bladder and bowels, and will instinctively leave the nest to defecate and urinate. In the wild, this behaviour helps to prevent disease and parasites such as intestinal worms (see pages 114–16), and also goes some way to maintaining hygienic conditions in the nest.

Toileting behaviour

Your kitten's digestive system is constantly producing waste, and – several times a day – his nervous system will send signals to his brain that start a pattern of instinctive behaviour that leads to the removal of the accumulated waste. The kitten will try to find a suitable place to go to the toilet, he will adopt the necessary body position, and he will go. But what will he consider to be an appropriate place?

When they first leave their nests to go to the toilet, most young kittens born in a domestic setting are faced with the choice of going on the floor or on a loose substrate such as cat litter (see pages 76–7).

When a kitten is very young, his mother takes care of his personal hygiene. By licking beneath his tail she stimulates him to urinate and defecate, and then eats what he produces.

Of the two options, almost all kittens seem to prefer to use cat litter, probably because they can then bury what they produce.

Although cats often leave their urine and faeces uncovered when they are away from their home territories – presumably to act as scent marks of their presence – most cover up any urine or faeces that they produce near the nest. Through experimentation and by watching their mother go to the toilet, most kittens brought up in the right sort of environment will train themselves to use a litter-tray (see pages 30–1).

However, as inappropriate toileting indoors is one of the most common cat-behaviour problems presented to behavioural experts, it is worth paying attention to the type of toilet-care products that you choose for your kitten, as well as to how you use them.

LITTER-TRAYS

There is nothing mysterious or magical about litter-trays. They are simply receptacles to prevent cat litter from being spread all over the floor!

Types of litter-tray

The simplest litter-trays are open-topped trays made of plastic. They usually come in several standard sizes, although some are deeper than others. Make sure that your kitten can easily walk into the litter-trays that you choose for him. In my view, the best types are those that are designed to be used with plastic liners: these will provide you with a simple and hygienic way of removing and discarding used litter (see page 77).

If your kitten is shy about going to the toilet, he may prefer a covered litter-tray. You can buy one of these, or you could simply turn an open-topped tray into an enclosed one by covering it with an upturned cardboard box with a hole cut in one side.

There are two basic types of litter-tray. The simplest tray is open (below), but many kittens are naturally shy about going to the toilet and may prefer to use a covered tray (right).

How many trays should you put out?

Your kitten will be naturally very particular about where he goes to the toilet. Squatting down to relieve himself is a very vulnerable time in his life, and he may be understandably wary about doing so in an open and public location. As you are not a cat, it will be impossible for you to decide on the site in your kitten's playroom that he would choose to use as a toilet, so a sensible option is to offer him more than one tray and to put the trays in different places.

At first you will need at least two trays. As soon as your kitten ventures beyond his playroom and into other parts of the house you may need more trays, so if you buy these at the start you will be better able to experiment with their locations, as well as with litter types (see page 76). Once you have identified your kitten's preferences, you can reduce the number of trays that you leave out. Any that are supplementary to his requirements can then be used as spares.

Tray positions

Initially, you should give your kitten a choice, as outlined above. The following are a few guidelines.
• Cats will often refuse to use litter-trays placed close to the area in which they eat, so avoid putting any of your kitten's trays near his food or water bowls.

- Avoid any busy locations such as near doors or on main thoroughfares through your house.
- Avoid open positions that provide little or no privacy.
- Cats often decide to sleep in litter-trays that are adjacent to their beds, so do not position any of your kitten's trays near favourite resting places.
- Avoid locations (such as behind doors) that may seem quiet and sheltered, but where your kitten may be unexpectedly disturbed while he is relieving himself.
- All litter-trays must be in locations to which your kitten can gain access 24 hours a day.
- If the only available places in your kitten's playroom seem rather exposed, consider offering him a covered litter-tray (see page 75). Some cats appear not to like being totally enclosed; in this case, try offering your kitten the choice of a customized tray with three tall cardboard sides, but no roof.

CAT LITTER

There are many options for this, including commercially manufactured products as well as natural substrates such as sand and soil. When you first bring your kitten home, fill all his trays with the litter to which he is accustomed: by doing so, you can be sure that – if he selects a particular tray to use – it is because of its location rather than its contents.

Once you have identified your kitten's preferred litter-tray locations, offer him a choice of different litter types in adjacent trays in the same spot. The majority of cat-owners find commercially prepared cat litters most convenient: in the UK, we spend £50 million each year on them. The older, more traditional litters are often clay-based, whereas more modern alternatives are made from materials such as recycled paper and even wood flour.

Visit a pet-accessory store in your area to identify what products are available where you live. If you would like further information on a product, you may need to contact the manufacturer concerned.

finely ground, natural-clay cat litter

wood-based, pelleted cat litter

traditional clay-based cat litter

Tips on choosing cat litter

The following are aspects to consider when choosing cat litter (some of these points have been identified by animal-behaviour experts involved in finding solutions to problems where cats have refused to use their litter-trays).

- Some cats seem to find certain pelleted cat litters uncomfortable to stand on, so allow your kitten to decide.
- Cat litters that contain chlorophyll are reported as being unattractive to some cats.
- Some litters may stain white fur.
- Certain litters – especially some wood-based varieties – may cling to long hair.
- Some litters are much more expensive than others.
- Some products are packed in either waterproof boxes or bags; these are both convenient to store and easy to use.
- Some litter materials are designed to minimize odours and keep trays smelling fresh. However, a litter-tray will only smell if it is left dirty, and some cats do not appear to like litters that release deodorizing scents when they are damp.
- Most cat litters produce 'clumps' when they become wet, to absorb the liquid, but some seem to do this more effectively than others. Those that 'clump' well may be more economical, as any soiled litter is easily separated from the clean material and the entire contents of the tray do not need to be thrown away so frequently.

Disposing of cat litter

If you do not choose to, or cannot, burn your kitten's used litter, you should check with your environmental-health authority as to how to dispose of it.

In many places, for instance, cat litter is considered clinical waste and should be dealt with accordingly. For health reasons, you should not bury litter in your garden or dispose of it in your sewerage system. Always wear rubber gloves when handling soiled litter.

If you are pregnant, you must leave the litter-tray duties to someone else.

Wearing a pair of rubber gloves, remove 'clumped' litter from your kitten's trays as necessary. Use a special scoop to do this, and be sure to wash it in disinfectant after use.

Cleaning your kitten's litter-trays

If you are too fastidious about cleaning your kitten's litter-trays he may stop using them, as the smell of previous urinations and defecation will attract him to use the trays again. However, most cats will also refuse to use a litter-tray that contains damp or dirty litter.

The frequency with which you need to clean out a litter-tray will obviously depend on how often your kitten uses it, and on the kind of litter that it contains. However, you should completely empty each tray and clean it using boiling water and veterinary disinfectant at least once a week. Remember to rinse out the tray very thoroughly to remove the smell of the cleaning and disinfecting solutions. Between these times, you should be able to remove soiled clumps of litter using a special litter scoop as and when necessary.

DEALING WITH INDOOR 'ACCIDENTS'

Even if you catch your kitten in the act of going to the toilet other than in his litter-tray, punishment will be pointless. What is more, if you frighten him in any way you may well make him more likely to go to the toilet in the wrong place again. Simply carry him to his litter-tray, and then go back and clean up the mess.

The smells of urine and faeces are natural signals that may stimulate your kitten to go to the toilet, so you must clean up carefully and thoroughly: remember that he will have a sense of smell far keener than yours. The only places that should smell of urine or faeces to him should be his litter-trays.

For hygiene reasons, start by removing the worst of the mess and cleaning the area with a proper veterinary disinfectant. Then scrub the area using a commercial cleaning solution specifically formulated to remove all the offending odours. In an emergency, a hot solution of biological washing-powder will do, followed by a scrub with surgical spirit or even some left-over vodka.

Once a week – or more frequently if necessary – thoroughly clean out your kitten's litter-trays. Using litter-tray liners will make this job less messy as well as more hygienic.

TOILETING OUTDOORS

As soon as your kitten has completed his vaccination course (see pages 120–1), you may decide to give him free or restricted access outdoors. In this case, he may choose to go to the toilet outside and will stop using his litter-trays indoors except in emergencies. Indeed, the majority of owners who allow their cats outdoors actively encourage them to go to the toilet there. This can be done by limiting a cat to one litter-tray inside the house, gradually moving it nearer to the cat flap, then to the other side of it and ultimately to a selected toileting spot in the garden.

Unfortunately, however, there is no guarantee if you do this that your kitten will continue to use the litter-tray outdoors, and he may well go anywhere in your garden or elsewhere if he has the opportunity. And is that fair on your neighbours?

Public awareness

The outdoor free-range toileting habits of pet cats are now becoming a serious issue of public concern. As it will be impossible to control where your kitten goes to the toilet outside, there are people who would argue that you should actually encourage him to continue using litter-trays, even if he has access outdoors. The decision is yours – at the moment – but it may not stay that way for ever.

Basic training

Despite what you may think, cats are quite capable of being trained: just like dogs, they respond to teaching that involves rewards. The reason why few owners train their cats is because it can be difficult to find suitable and effective rewards to offer them. In addition, although it is certainly possible to train your kitten to fetch your slippers, it is unlikely that you will think it appropriate for him to do so. After all, isn't that what dogs are for?

Why train your kitten?

You may wish to teach your kitten to come back when you call, or to discourage him from certain activities such as opening cupboard doors or jumping on to work surfaces. To achieve these things, you will need to understand some of the basics of how he learns.

Instrumental learning

This is one of the main ways in which your kitten will learn to repeat certain actions. The principle is that, if your kitten is immediately rewarded for performing a certain behaviour in response to a particular situation or stimulus, he will be more likely to perform the same behaviour if he encounters that situation again.

For example, if he walks into the kitchen, jumps on to the work surface and comes face to face with a tasty bit of tuna, he is more likely to jump on to the work surface when he walks into the kitchen on another occasion. The sights, sounds and smells of the kitchen constitute the 'stimulus', jumping is the 'behaviour' and his 'reward' is the tuna.

Imitating natural behaviour

You will find that it is much easier to teach your kitten to carry out actions that are similar to natural behaviour that he would perform instinctively. For instance, even without your help he will probably learn to open doors using a front paw, because it is a similar action to the 'scooping' that he will engage in as part of object play (see page 83). On the other hand, it would be almost impossible to teach him to open a door using his mouth.

If you have another cat, you will also discover that your kitten can learn to do things without the use of rewards. For instance, if he sees your other cat use the cat flap, he will probably walk straight through it himself. Your role will then be to stop him if he has not completed his vaccination course!

Teaching your kitten to come to you

As you can see from the previous example, your kitten will learn to do things that he finds rewarding even when you are not there to act as his teacher. If you wish to teach him something specific – such as to come when called – you need to arrange that the stimulus (you saying the word 'COME'), his behaviour (coming to you) and the reward (perhaps a small piece of food that he finds tasty) all occur at the right time and in the right way to ensure that learning takes place.

To achieve this, rather than attaching a lead to your kitten's collar and dragging him towards you when you ask him to come, it will be much more effective – and much less traumatic for your kitten – if you wait until he is coming towards you of his own free will. As he moves closer, keep saying 'COME', and then, when he arrives, immediately reward him. Later on, you can go on to adapt this simple piece of training to a more complex task, such as teaching your kitten to use his cat flap (see pages 86–7).

Further training

With a great deal of patience, you should be able to teach your kitten to do all kinds of things using the same principle. Taking part in well-planned training exercises will also have the advantage of helping to stimulate his mind: for instance, kittens kept indoors often benefit from the experience of learning simple tricks such as 'fetch' games.

WHAT MAKES A GOOD REWARD?

The most effective training rewards for your kitten will be those items that he anticipates with eagerness, or that he makes some effort to obtain. He may respond well to different rewards on different occasions. The following are a few suggestions for suitable rewards.

• Pieces of highly palatable food (if you use anything other than your kitten's normal food, these should be very small so as not to upset the balance of his diet).

• The opportunity to investigate a new object.

• Your attention.

• The chance to play (see pages 83–5).

• Access to a favourite resting place.

Giving rewards

A reward must be given at the same time as your kitten carries out desired behaviour, as a delay of even one second will weaken its effect. When you start to train your kitten, you should reward him every time he responds correctly. Once he masters something, you only need to reward him occasionally.

What about punishment?

You may think that, if your kitten learns about good behaviour through associating pleasant rewards with desirable actions on his part, the simplest way to stop any bad behaviour is to ensure that he associates it with unpleasant punishments. In fact, this is wrong: the opposite of a reward is the absence of a reward.

If your kitten is about to dig his claws into your new sofa, shouting at him or smacking him may stop him on that occasion, but he is likely to do it again when you are not there. All you will achieve by punishing him in this way will be to damage your relationship with him.

However, there will be occasions – such as when your kitten jumps on to a piece of furniture or opens a cupboard that is out of bounds – when you will have to interrupt him in some way. Whenever you think about doing so, bear the following points in mind.

The clatter of these training disks landing near your kitten when he is indulging in some unacceptable behaviour will break his concentration. You should use such disks only when really necessary.

• The degree of interruption must be exactly right. A stern 'NO' may stop your kitten from scratching the sofa, but may be ineffective in another situation.
• As with a reward, an interruption must be carried out immediately if it is to be meaningful.
• The best interruptions are often mild ones that will simply startle or surprise. For instance, making a hissing sound will quickly distract most cats.
• Wherever and whenever possible, try to think of appropriate distractions that will be seen by your kitten as 'acts of God'. In this way, he will perceive that the interruption is a direct result of his behaviour rather than thinking of you as a strict disciplinarian. Good examples are a quick and sudden dousing spurt of water from a plant sprayer, directed from some distance away, or the clattering of a ring of metal disks carefully thrown to land near your kitten. However, you will have to be clever to fool him for very long.

When using a plant sprayer to prevent undesirable behaviour, stand as far from your kitten as you can so that, if possible, he does not associate the dousing with you.

Your kitten's lifestyle

Left to their own devices, cats like to make up their own minds about what they do, and when and where they do it. Fortunately, they seem to adapt easily to the different environments and lifestyles that are imposed on them, and this is perhaps one of the reasons why cats make such good pets for such a wide range of people. However, you should never take your kitten's flexible attitude for granted.

Taking life as it comes

The quality of your kitten's life will be more important to him than the quantity of it. After all, he will not worry about the future: like all cats, he will focus on the present. For him, life is to be taken day by day.

Over the next weeks and months your kitten will become a much-loved member of your family, and will grow both physically and mentally into an adult cat. Although he may be wild at heart, he has to learn about living with people, but he should also have fun.

Unlike most pet cats, an African wild cat has to cope with an ever-changing lifestyle. He may not survive as long as a pet cat, but his life will almost certainly be more stimulating.

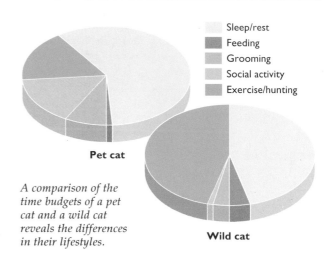

Sleep/rest
Feeding
Grooming
Social activity
Exercise/hunting

Pet cat

Wild cat

A comparison of the time budgets of a pet cat and a wild cat reveals the differences in their lifestyles.

Cats in the wild

In the wild your kitten's ancestor, the African wild cat (see pages 8–9), leads an unpredictable kind of life. For him, there is no guarantee of a warm, sheltered bed and a nourishing meal each and every day, and he is constantly stressed and stimulated by the world in which he lives. Sudden changes in the weather, rivalry with other animals and the inherent dangers involved in hunting are just some of the hardships with which a wild cat has to cope, but his body and his brain are well-suited to such a lifestyle.

Cats at home

Pet cats, on the other hand, often lead very predictable lives. Quite naturally, we tend to feel it is necessary to protect our pet kittens as if they were young, helpless babies, even when they are fully grown adult cats. Of course, some kinds of pet cat require a great deal of cosseting because their coat type or body shape is far removed from what would be required for them to survive in the wild on their own. And who knows what domestication and human interference in their breeding has really done to their brains?

However, even if your kitten is a glamorous breed such as a Persian, do not just assume that he needs – or indeed wishes – to be constantly waited upon and wrapped in cotton wool. Throughout his life, you should try to ensure that your kitten is continually exposed to new and stimulating experiences that will broaden his horizons.

Allowing your kitten outdoors

In comparison with other kinds of pet animal that are kept caged, tethered or tanked, kittens and adult cats who are allowed unlimited access outdoors have an enviable degree of freedom. If I were a pet I would wish to be a free-ranging cat, because I would be able to choose my own way of life. Some kittens and cats who enjoy a free-choice lifestyle elect to spend most of their time indoors, even though their cat flaps are left open; others seem to prefer the excitement and challenges offered by the great outdoors.

Keeping your kitten indoors

Even without any external pressure to do so, you may elect for your own very good reasons to restrict your kitten's freedom, perhaps because of concerns for his health and safety. You may decide only to allow him outdoors at certain times, or possibly to limit his access outside to a fenced enclosure (see pages 88–9). You may even keep your cat permanently inside your house or flat, possibly because you cannot give him access to a safe outdoor area.

   If you adopt any of these management alternatives, you must also accept the challenging responsibility of providing your kitten with the option to engage in man-made, home-based activities that will offer the same kind of mental and physical stimulation that he would experience outdoors.

   For instance, you will need to invent games that challenge your kitten's stalking and hunting instincts, and to provide him with climbing and other exercise

The more you understand and address your kitten's mental and physical needs, the more he will enjoy life. All kinds of things will stimulate his curiosity and athletic prowess.

opportunities to stress his athletic body. In one recent study, a well-fed, neutered female pet cat, given free access outdoors, was discovered to patrol a territory of just under half a hectare; while in the Australian bush some female cats have been found to have home ranges of over 150 hectares. Bearing in mind statistics such as these, it is hardly surprising that cats kept indoors more commonly become overweight than their outdoor rambling relatives.

A stimulating environment

Most important of all, if you keep your kitten indoors you must ensure that his lifestyle is at least slightly unpredictable by varying the games that you play together and the toys that you offer him. Of course, you may go to the effort of providing a wonderful climbing frame, only to find that your kitten ignores it. That is fine: he had the choice to climb it and he decided not to do so, but you will have to go back to the drawing-board and come up with something else.

YOUR ROLE AS AN OWNER

Feeding your kitten a good diet, giving him a place in which to rest his head, grooming him and attending to his medical needs are important steps towards keeping him alive for as long as possible. But if this is all that you do for him, will he be happy?

   Be prepared to break with tradition, and dare to be a different kind of cat-owner. Plan a full, varied and fun life for your kitten, whether he is a free-roamer or is restricted indoors. Experiment with his lifestyle, and keep trying new things. When appropriate, and as often as possible, give your kitten the freedom to make a few decisions for himself.

   Most of us would agree that the worst aspect about owning a cat is that he will not live as long as we would like. It is up to you to ensure that, while he is with you, your cat gets the most from his relatively short life.

The indoor kitten

You should make the decision as to whether you will keep your kitten permanently indoors before you bring him home. Of course you can change your mind, but it is likely to be more difficult for you and more traumatic for your kitten if you allow him outside after completing his first vaccination course (see pages 120–1), and then decide to keep him as an indoor pet. A young kitten who has not experienced life outdoors is likely to adjust better to having his movements restricted than an older kitten who already knows about life on the other side of the cat flap.

Important considerations

Keeping a kitten indoors is not a decision to be made lightly. The following are some aspects to think about.
• The need that all cats share for the kind of physical and mental stimulation that an outdoor lifestyle offers.
• The responsibility that you have as a cat-owner to offer your kitten as many lifestyle choices as you can. Remember that there may also be the option of giving him restricted access outdoors (see pages 88–9).
• Think about the kind of kitten that you have chosen, and his suitability to an indoor lifestyle. For instance,

certain longer-haired cats, such as Persians, have coats that are not well-adapted to scrambling through dense undergrowth, while some sturdy, active and highly independent breeds could become very frustrated by indoor confinement (see pages 44–6).

LIFE INDOORS

Even older kittens who have unlimited access outdoors should come inside to sleep, eat and play. With a little guidance from their owners, they may even return home to go to the toilet (see page 77).

Kittens who are kept indoors must also exercise their bodies and their minds. It will be impossible to formulate an appropriate indoor-management policy for your kitten without having a basic understanding of some of his natural physical and behavioural needs.

Sleep

Cats are competent sleepers! At least eight and up to 12 hours a day is the general rule, but older cats may snooze for as many as 16 hours a day. This does not mean that cats are lazy: they are simply obeying nature's golden rule that a well-fed carnivore should

---

SCRATCHING AND CLAW SHARPENING

Your kitten will have a natural desire to claw at specially selected objects in his environment (see page 39). You should encourage and train him to use special scratching posts, of which there are many different types available. Some indoor climbing frames even have scratching stations incorporated into their design.

The following are a few hints and tips on choosing scratching posts and encouraging your kitten to use them.

• Offer your kitten a choice of several scratching posts of different sizes, shapes and textures. You will soon discover which type he prefers.

• You can make your own scratching posts from natural objects such as bark-covered logs, or by wrapping a length of natural-fibre rope around a short piece of fence-post and then screwing it securely to a wooden base.

• Avoid a scratching post that is covered in fabric (such as carpet) that your kitten may also find elsewhere in your house.

• Some cats seem to enjoy scratching at low objects or even those lying flat on the floor, but you should also give your kitten the opportunity to indulge in some high-level scratching. Make sure that at least one of the scratching posts that you offer him is taller than he is long when he is standing up on his hindlegs with his body and forelegs at full stretch.

• Despite being offered a choice of different scratching posts, your kitten may still claw at other household furnishings. If you catch him doing so, distract him (see page 79) and carry him to one of his proper scratching posts. Attaching one of his favourite toys – such as a plastic ball – to a scratching post and letting it dangle invitingly from the top may be a good way of encouraging your kitten to use the post.

keep himself out of sight, both to remain hidden from rivals of his own species and to avoid scaring away potential prey. As the majority of pet cats are offered a regular and plentiful supply of food, many cats may be close to a soporific state almost permanently.

Unlike people, cats do not do all their sleeping in a single period. Instead, they really do 'cat-nap', splitting their sleep into several bouts spread over 24 hours. They are most active at dawn and dusk, and are most likely to sleep in the middle of the night and the middle of the day.

In one respect, a cat's sleep is very like ours. It consists of alternating periods of light sleep, in which the cat sleeps peacefully but from which he is easily woken; and deeper sleep, when he is much less easy to wake. The deep sleep is known as 'paradoxical' sleep as, although the cat is completely limp most of the time, his whiskers, tail or paws may occasionally twitch, or his eyes may flicker. This is just what people do when they are dreaming, so we can speculate that cats also dream when they are sleeping.

For restful sleep, your kitten will need the following.

• A choice of sleeping locations where he will not be disturbed. Some should be in warm spots, and some should be off the ground.

• A choice of bedding materials.

• The chance to reach his sleeping places 24 hours a day, so that he can 'cat-nap' when he wishes.

Food

Feral cats hunt and feed several times a day because their natural food is concentrated in small amounts and their digestive systems work relatively quickly.

Pet cats also appear to have a need to hunt, even if they are not hungry. In fact, many cats will set off on a hunting expedition immediately after eating a convenience meal offered by their owners. A well-fed house cat allowed free access outdoors may well spend a quarter of each day hunting. An active cat weighing

This kitten is enjoying a game with his toy mouse, but he will also have fun with something as straightforward as a screwed-up piece of paper. Offer your kitten a variety of play objects, but ration him to just one or two at a time to maintain his interest.

3.5 kg (8 lb) needs to take in about 300 calories a day. As an average mouse provides about 30 calories of energy, it would be fair to assume that a cat living on a diet of mice would need 10 meals in every 24 hours. Most pet cats fed on prepared cat foods (see pages 58–60) also prefer to eat many small meals during the day. Having a number of small meals is especially important for a kitten, who will find it difficult to eat enough if he is only fed once or twice a day. In terms of his food, your kitten will need the following.

• Access to one or more foods that will fulfil all his nutritional needs (see pages 54–67).

• A number of small meals each day.

• The opportunity to use his predatory hunting instincts and skills on real or imaginary prey (see below and page 85).

Play

Kittens indulge in three basic types of play.

Object play • This involves interaction with inanimate objects. When confronted with new objects, a kitten begins by investigating them with his eyes, nose, tongue and paws, and then goes on to poke, bat, grasp or toss them in the air. In all, over 10 types of object-play behaviour have been identified (see page 85). Recent research has indicated that well-orchestrated object play stimulates cats in a manner very similar to their natural hunting activities, and so may reduce a kitten's in-built predatory desires. Kittens spend most time involved in object play at around 16 weeks old. After this, the amount of this kind of play indulged in by a particular kitten will depend on his character and personality.

Locomotor play • This consists of running, rolling, jumping and climbing. During their first year, kittens are naturally very playful creatures. For instance, if provided with a climbing frame (see page 84), a kitten will spend considerably more time clambering on it than an adult cat would do.

Social play • This consists of interaction between kittens. To an outside observer such games might look like fights, but most play bouts of this kind do end amicably. Kittens are most actively involved in social play between the ages of nine and 14 weeks.

TOYS AND OTHER PLAY ITEMS

You should either buy or make a whole range of play objects for your kitten. These do not all need to be highly sophisticated: perhaps the best, simplest and the most successful cat toy of all time is a screwed-up piece of paper.

Safety first

It almost goes without saying that all toys that you make should be strong and safe, as your kitten may become quite ferocious while playing and will certainly try to dismember a toy using his claws and mouth. Any toy that you buy should be well-packaged and labelled with full instructions for use. Avoid those that are sold loose, and test the strength of all toys yourself before offering them to your kitten.

Keeping your kitten amused

Do not just imagine that all you have to do to satisfy your kitten's play needs is to offer him three or four toys and then let him get on with it. Kittens become bored very quickly with toys.

Despite recent scientific studies on this subject, experts still do not understand why kittens and cats seem to be endlessly fascinated with real (dead) mice but quickly tire of toy versions. However, they are in no doubt that – if a kitten is to get the most from playing with his toys – he will need the help of his owner. You will soon discover which games your kitten enjoys playing, and which tend to bore him.

Do not be disappointed if your kitten is not as impressed by some of his playthings as you are. This older kitten's owners have bought him a wonderful activity centre, but he is much more interested in the plastic ball hanging beneath the top platform.

AN ADVENTURE PLAYGROUND

If your kitten lives permanently indoors, you should provide him with a fun area to stimulate locomotor play (see page 83). The following are a few ideas.

• Put out cardboard boxes of different sizes for your kitten to climb in, on and over.

• Place cushions on the floor for him to hide behind.

• Turn tough paper bags into tunnels by opening them up at both ends.

• Arrange rugs to form tunnels and hiding places.

• The ultimate play item for an indoor kitten is a climbing frame or activity centre (see left). There are many different types available: the largest reach from floor to ceiling and have several platforms incorporating sleeping and feeding areas.

WARNING

Never leave your kitten with wool or any other kind of thread that is either loose or attached to a toy. Kittens have backward-pointing, hard spines on their tongues, and once they have a piece of thread in their mouths it can be very difficult for them to spit it out. Sewing thread with a needle still attached to it is particularly dangerous, and is a well-known hazard to kittens.

Hints and tips on toys

As your kitten grows older and naturally less playful, he will rely more and more on you to initiate games, and will be less likely to want to play on his own. You will therefore need to be prepared to put even more time and effort into keeping him mentally stimulated and well-entertained.

The following are some useful ways of keeping your kitten interested in his toys.

• Offer him toys that are likely to stimulate his play behaviour (see below and right).

• Make sure that your kitten has a whole range of toys stored away. Only offer him one or two of these to play with at a time, and keep replacing them with different ones.

• Buy toys for him in a variety of different shapes, colours and textures.

• When playing with your kitten, do not allow him to become frustrated. If he looks as if he may be growing confused or frantic, change the game.

• Be ingenious when playing with your kitten and trying to stimulate his natural behaviour. In the wild, a mouse will try very hard to get away from a cat, moving quickly and hiding. He will not attach a piece of string to his head, throw it over a branch and then dangle himself in front of the cat's nose!

• Experiment with everyday objects. These can be as complex or as simple as you like: for instance, some kittens are fascinated by the plastic screw-tops from milk containers. The more variety, the better.

Well-known object-play behaviour

The chase • In this behaviour, a kitten runs after a fast-moving object. Toys that may be rolled or pulled along the floor at speed will stimulate this reaction. My cat Gorbachov loves chasing nuggets of his dinner that I flick across the room for him. He can even catch nuggets from quite a distance away by using his front paws like baseball gloves.

The pounce • Here, a kitten crouches with his head on the ground and then treads up and down with his hindlegs before suddenly leaping forwards. Your kitten may do this to everyday objects – such as a leaf on the carpet – and some kittens will do it to apparently invisible objects. Dragging a toy along the ground, then stopping it suddenly before continuing to move it in a jerking manner often stimulates kittens to pounce.

The bat • Using either of his front paws, a kitten will swipe at a dangling object or poke at one that is on the ground. Suitable objects include ping-pong balls, screwed-up paper and any safe toys – such as mouse-shaped ones – that may be dangled.

The grasp • In this action, a kitten will hold an object between his front paws or in his mouth. He may grasp the object in his mouth and then release it by shaking his head: this is known as the toss.

The scoop • With this behaviour, a kitten picks up an object with one of his front paws by curving the paw under the object; he will then grasp it firmly with his claws.

Providing your kitten with the right kinds of toys will help to stimulate different aspects of his natural play behaviour. This kitten is practising the one-paw scoop on his toy mouse, an action that cats often use on real mice to foil their escape.

The outdoor kitten

The great outdoors can offer a kitten the mental and physical stimulation that is difficult to create inside a house. If at all possible, you should let your kitten experience life outside from the time that he completes his first vaccination course (see pages 120–1).

A CAT FLAP

The great advantage of a cat flap is that it will allow your kitten the freedom to come and go without you having to open an ordinary door or a window for him. There are many different types of flap, some of which are much more sophisticated than others.

Your kitten will quickly become used to a cat flap with a little encouragement and help from you. When you first fit the flap, prop its door open securely with something solid that will not fall over if your kitten brushes against it. A frightening experience early on – such as the door suddenly slamming behind him or on top of him – may make him very reluctant to go near it again for some time.

Let your kitten take things at his own pace. Initially, he may spend time astride the flap, half-in and half-out, while he surveys the world around him. As he grows more confident he may make a dash for cover somewhere nearby in the garden, although a sudden noise will soon make him dart back inside.

Types of cat flap

The basic cat flap is simply a door on a hinge, which will flap open in either direction. This type of flap is inexpensive and easy to fit. A two-way locking device is a good idea, as this will allow you some control over your kitten's movements: for example, allowing him in but not out (this will be useful if you prefer to keep him in at night, as well as keeping other cats out).

A more sophisticated cat flap will allow access only to your kitten, using a special key that is attached to his collar. This key will trigger a mechanism on the cat flap itself when the kitten approaches it. A cat flap of this type will be ideal if you live in a neighbourhood of cats who like to visit their friends' homes.

Choosing a cat flap

• Look for a cat flap with a door that seals well and will not blow open in the wind.
• Make sure that the door on the flap is transparent. It will be important to your kitten to check whether the coast is clear before he sticks his head through.

• If you opt for a key-operated cat flap, make sure that it comes with a spare 'key' in case your kitten loses his collar while out on an adventure.
• It is worth paying a little extra for a very sturdy, well-made cat flap. With continual use, it is surprising how quickly a less solid flap may become worn out.

Positioning a cat flap

There are many options for this. The most obvious position is in an outside door, although some cat flaps are specially designed to be fitted into cavity walls and are supplied with a tunnel section to act as a sleeve through the brickwork. My cat Gorbachov has his flap in place of a small windowpane: I removed the glass and replaced it with a piece of Perspex with a hole cut in it to accommodate the flap.

The following are some points to consider when positioning a cat flap for your kitten.
• Think about where your kitten would want his cat flap to be. Will he get a good panoramic view of the world outside through it, so that he can check for any potential hazards and dangers? For instance, outside Gorbachov's flap is a large windowsill on to which he can walk; this provides him with a good vantage point, and doubles as an escape ledge if he is being

When first training your kitten to use his cat flap, you can try encouraging him to walk through it by placing his food bowl on the other side of the flap.

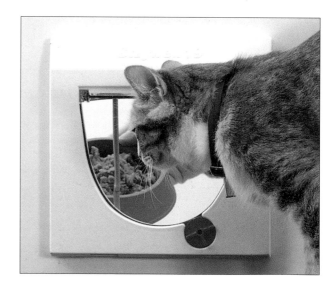

Perhaps the most obvious place for a cat flap is in an outside door, but positioning it in a wall or in a piece of Perspex used to replace a pane of glass is a good alternative.

chased by another cat. Your kitten's flap should be a secure bolthole to which he can gain access quickly and easily if he feels that he may be in danger.

• If your kitten has just been out exploring, you may not want him walking straight into your living-room. He may also make the area around the inside of his cat flap filthy, especially during the wet winter months. Not only will he come skipping in with muddy paws, but he is also very likely to scent-rub the walls and any furniture close to the flap as soon as he comes in.

• The cat flap should be within the part of your house to which you allow your kitten unsupervised access, as you may not always be about when he comes back from a trip outdoors.

• If you have a dog, make sure that the flap is not in a place where the dog can prevent your kitten from coming in. My dog Jessie adores Gorbachov, but finds the appearance of his head through the cat flap an irresistible cue for a game. Occasionally, Jessie's over-enthusiastic welcome is enough to make Gorbachov retreat back through his cat flap at high speed!

• If possible, the flap should be on the safest side of your house, and certainly away from a busy road.

• Whatever location you choose, make sure that you fit the flap at an appropriate height. Most kittens can cope with a cat flap at a height suitable for an average adult cat. The bottom edge of the flap should be no more

than about 15 cm (6 in) from the floor (or windowsill if the flap is in a window).

• Do not fit a cat flap in a door between your house and an attached garage. This is a fire door, and cutting a hole in it will reduce its fire-stopping properties.

• Whether the cat flap is fitted in a door or window, make sure that a would-be intruder cannot reach through it to undo a lock and get into your house.

Disadvantages of a cat flap

• One common problem with a cat flap is that other cats in your neighbourhood may use it to come into your house – and your kitten's territory. He may find such unexpected visits very traumatic. Intruders are also often the cause of behavioural problems such as urine-spraying indoors by a resident cat. For this reason, magnetic key-operated cat flaps (see opposite) are particularly useful in areas of high cat populations.

• Some cats appear to develop insecurity problems even if intruders have not made any uninvited visits, as they appear to feel that a permanently open cat flap makes their territory vulnerable. This is really quite understandable: how would you feel going to sleep at night knowing that your front door is unlocked?

• Having free access outdoors may encourage your kitten to stay outside for longer periods and wander further from home. This may be especially true if you offer him a dry food on a 'self-service' basis, as he will not feel the need to return home at set mealtimes.

WALKING YOUR KITTEN

If you are not able to offer your kitten free access outdoors but would still like him to get plenty of fresh air, you may think about buying a harness for him to wear so that you can walk him outside on a lead. In theory this is a splendid idea; in practice it can be difficult to train many cats to accept being restricted in such a way. However, I have it on good authority that some cats – particularly those of the Siamese and Burmese breeds – take to it like dogs.

Make sure if you buy a harness that it fits your kitten securely, and do not venture outside until both you and he are fully accustomed to the experience inside your house. Even if your kitten seems to be very happy in a harness and on a lead, I would not recommend that you venture into public places with him. If he were suddenly frightened he could become frantic, and you could be badly scratched and injured through trying to control him. If in the turmoil you were to let go of his lead, you might never see him again.

AN OUTDOOR ENCLOSURE

Some suppliers build cat runs to order, which will arrive ready-to-assemble. However, if you are a DIY enthusiast you may prefer to build one yourself. The simplest designs look very much like cages, but with a little creativity and careful planning a cat run could become an attractive feature of your garden.

Building a cat run

If you intend to build your own run, it will be worth visiting cat-owning families who have already built runs, as they will be able to give you some valuable hints and tips. The staff at your vet centre may know of owners with cat runs in your area, or, failing this, you could contact cat magazines to see if they know of anyone. Cat runs are becoming increasingly popular because of owners' current fears about road dangers, contagious cat viruses and theft, so many magazines are running features on them.

The base of the run may consist of concrete (shaped to drain water) or grass, or a mixture of both. Soft gravel is also a good option. Before going ahead with the construction of a run, check whether you need planning permission in your area. In addition, if you do not own your house you should make sure that your plans are acceptable to your landlord.

Furnishing a cat run

Your kitten's run should be a place in which he can stimulate his body and his brain. You should therefore aim not only to give him as much space as possible, but also to ensure that the run is properly furnished. It should be sheltered from prevailing wind and rain, and – as cats love to sunbathe – part of the run should trap the sun if possible on clear, fine days.

WARNING

Poisoning in cats is extremely rare in my experience, but there is no point in tempting fate. Your kitten's freedom will be restricted in a run, so it is fair to assume that he may become more inquisitive of his immediate surroundings than he might otherwise be. As a result, he may be tempted to chew, lick or even eat unusual objects. You must therefore make sure that no wooden surfaces to which your kitten may have access have been painted with creosote, either on your side or on that of your neighbours.

It will also be wise to check with your vet centre to find out whether a plant that you would like to put in your kitten's run could be potentially poisonous to him before you go ahead.

At the absolute minimum, your kitten's enclosure should include the following.
• A warm, weatherproof cabin or den.
• A covered toileting area, housing a litter-tray.
• Areas that will be shaded from the sun.
• Platforms for observation and sleeping.
• Entertainment in the form of a tree trunk to climb and scratch, and toys (some hanging, others loose). Vary the contents of the enclosure, as an unpredictable environment will be much more stimulating.

Optional extras

• A catnip plant or two: many cats adore the smell of this herb, and several varieties are available.
• Other plants and shrubs, although you must be careful to avoid those poisonous to cats (see above).
• Grass: some cats enjoy eating this – perhaps to aid digestion, although there is no proof that it does so.

MAKING YOUR GARDEN CAT-PROOF

Cats are remarkably capable escape artists. If you intend to make your garden completely secure, you should bear in mind the following points.

• An average adult cat may be able to clamber through a hole in a fence that is just 10 cm (4 in) wide, so check carefully around the perimeter of your garden.

• Cats can climb most fences with ease; vertical brick walls are more difficult if there are no footholds. The boundary structure should be at least 3 m (10 ft) in height with wire-mesh fencing angled inwards on top and a narrow horizontal net roof attached to it.

• Gates are an obvious escape route. Those made from some type of mesh, rather than a solid material, will enable anyone entering your garden to check the whereabouts of your kitten before venturing in. A set of double gates is ideal, so that the outer door can be closed before the inner one is opened.

• Trees with branches that overhang your boundary fence could provide your kitten with a high-rise walkway into the next-door garden. Be prepared to prune back or remove any extensive vegetation that your kitten could use as a ladder or a bridge.

For a number of reasons, more and more owners are choosing to restrict their cats' outdoor activities to a secure enclosure. If you decide to do the same, you should consider the overall size, construction and layout of your kitten's enclosure very carefully. It should be as big as possible, totally secure (any entrances should have double doors or gates) and be made of safe materials. Its interior design should offer your kitten a stimulating environment with plenty of activity and other options, including sheltered and open places, ground-level hideaways and high-level platforms. If you have a small walled garden or yard, you may be able to turn the whole area into a suitable enclosure for your kitten.

Out and about

When a cat goes out through his cat flap, he will generally have two things on his mind: other cats and hunting. Most cats who are allowed access outdoors have split personalities. Indoors they are affectionate, interactive pets, but as soon as they venture through their cat flaps they become solitary hunters with no need for company of any kind.

If you offer your kitten access outdoors, you will no doubt be fascinated and perhaps even concerned about what he gets up to when he is out of the house. However, unless you fit a radio-transmitter to his collar you are unlikely ever to discover exactly where he ventures, with whom he interacts or how long he spends in any given place. He will have his favourite haunts and will probably tread the same paths around his territory, but most of his routes and destinations will remain well-kept secrets.

In order to give you a glimpse of what life for a cat is like on the other side of the cat flap, the following is an account of a typical excursion by a one-year-old neutered male cat, living in a neighbourhood of many cats. The cat's name is William.

A DAY IN THE LIFE OF WILLIAM

Before heading off down the garden, William sniffs the brickwork surrounding his cat flap. From time to time a tom cat is known to pass by: he may have done so recently, and may even have attempted to get through the flap to steal some of William's food. Entire (unneutered) male cats can roam over large areas searching for mates; even in towns, they may travel 1 km (½ mile) or more from their home bases (see opposite). Such cats will routinely check their territories for telltale signs of potential rivals, and will spray their pungent urine around the territories of other cats. William is very quick to detect that the local tom cat has left his calling card right outside his back door!

William's owners are already out of sight and out of mind. As he moves away down the garden he keeps a wary look-out for an older neutered male who lives in the house next door. This male was in residence before William was even born and – like all young cats – William respects the territory of his older, stronger and wiser neighbour.

Finding scent marks

While climbing a tree to get to the top of the wall at the bottom of his garden, William discovers two scent marks deposited on prominent twigs, from the cheek-glands of two of his neighbours. He 'gapes' as he sniffs these to identify the cats responsible (see page 33).

One mark is from the male next door but the scent is stale, suggesting that he passed this way several hours earlier, possibly on his way to his favoured hunting ground on nearby wasteland. The other was left by a neutered female – also a one-year-old – who is sunbathing on a garage roof. There is no rivalry between these two, so William passes by undeterred.

William knows that he will shortly have to pass his adversary's territory. To remain as inconspicuous as possible, he follows a well-hidden route between a wall and a hedge, taking care not to rub his cheeks on the brickwork or foliage, as any scent marks that he may leave behind will betray his presence.

William is a one-year-old, neutered male cat. He is a typical moggie and has a lifestyle likely to be similar to that of most pet cats given free access by their owners to roam outdoors.

William's outdoor territory

- ☐ William's territory
- ☐ Female cat's territory
- **1** William's house
- **2** Female cat's house
- **3** Older tom cat's house
- **4** Female cat sunbathing on garage roof
- **5** Wall
- **6** Dry ditch

This map shows William's territory and how it relates to that of the female cat who lives across the road. The outdoor activities of cats are fascinating, but remain a mystery to most owners.

60 metres (80 yards)

Going hunting

William's aim is to reach the corner of a park, situated not far from his own house. A low wall provides him with a vantage point, from which he can scan a dry ditch and a shrubby area where birds and mice often feed. A cat whose choice of hunting sites is limited will usually hunt in this way, remaining motionless for hours while he waits for prey to appear. If he has greater freedom to move around, he may move swiftly and silently from one area to another, hoping to find his prey out in the open.

William is well-fed by his owners and does not need to catch his own food, but – quite naturally – he enjoys the mental and physical stimulation of the hunt. He is game to have a go, but he is an inexperienced hunter and returns home with nothing more than thoughts of what could have been.

Taking prey home

If he had caught anything, William would probably have carried his prey home. Owners often mistake this as a sign that their cats are treating their human family as if they were kittens needing to be fed. In fact, the simplest explanation is that cats like to eat their catch in safety. However, most cats prefer commercial cat food to their natural prey, and so abandon anything they have caught as soon as they have carried it home.

SIX YEARS LATER

Now middle-aged in cat terms, William has much greater freedom of movement than he had when he was just one year old.

The male from next door died two years previously and was not replaced, so William gradually took over his territory. At first, he spent a lot of time basking in his former rival's favourite spot near his front door, almost as if to seal his right to ownership. He now routinely urine-sprays on prominent objects around his hunting range although, because he is neutered, his urine is less pungent than that of an entire tom cat.

A 14-week-old male kitten, now living in a house across the road, keeps well out of William's way.

Other residents

William now shares his house with two females: one of five years old and the other – her daughter – of two years old. This pair spend much of their time together, which is to be expected as cat society is based upon liaisons between closely related females.

William keeps his distance, even though he is their great-uncle and great-great-uncle respectively. Cats do not instinctively know to whom they are related: they learn this in their first eight weeks. Cats who become friends are usually those who lived together when they were four to eight weeks old (see pages 30–5).

Most young pet cats are athletic and agile animals, who are well-designed for short-burst dashes across country in pursuit of their prey.

CAT HUNTING

The detrimental effect of cat hunting on wildlife is currently a major area of public concern – more so in some parts of the world than in others. Wildlife experts often suspect pet, feral and farm cats of causing damage to local wild-animal populations through their hunting activities and, as a result, the subject is being studied in great detail.

To date, we know most about the kinds of wild animal that are actually eaten by cats. We know much less about those that are caught and then discarded, although ongoing research is likely to improve our understanding of this contentious subject.

How does cat hunting affect wildlife?

The following are some of the facts that have been discovered so far.
• Mammals appear to be more common prey items than birds. This confirms the notion that cats are specialized predators of small mammals.
• In North America and Europe, the common and field voles appear to be the mammals most favoured as hunting victims by cats. Young rabbits and hares are also popular.
• Mice and young rats are less commonly eaten, perhaps because they are less palatable than voles. However, pet cats frequently bring these creatures home and then discard them.
• Shrews appear to be unpalatable to cats.

• In North America – but not in Europe – ground squirrels and chipmunks are common prey items.
• In Australasia, rabbits, rats and mice together with small marsupials and other native mammals are taken.
• Birds – particularly seabirds – are important prey items to cats who live on islands.
• Insects, spiders, crustaceans and molluscs are also eaten by cats.

Reducing hunting instincts

Playing appropriate games with your kitten indoors that stimulate his natural hunting instincts may be a very effective way of reducing his desire to hunt for real when he is outdoors (see page 85). Equally, such games could sharpen up his timing and accuracy!

THE HUNTING CAT

It is very difficult to assess the true impact that cat-hunting activities have on wild-animal populations. This is because relatively little is known about the dining habits of other predators, or about other causes of death in the wild animals on whom cats prey.

Cat predation of songbirds is often noticed because it takes place during the day, whereas most hunting of mammals goes on at night. What is more, in my experience, there are plenty of keen birdwatchers about, but perhaps fewer small-mammal enthusiasts. Some experts believe that it is unlikely that cats have any greater impact on small-bird populations than other predators would do if their numbers were not artificially controlled, but opinion is divided on this.

CAT FIGHTS

Cats are territorial animals. They will mark their own territories using a combination of urine, faeces, body scents and claw marks, and they will also try to defend their territories from others.

Inevitably, the territories of some individuals will overlap in places. The cats concerned may fight each other for territorial rights, although most will avoid fighting if possible. After all, when two cats set about each other with claw and tooth, even the ultimate victor will not leave the scene unscathed.

Feline hierarchies

Fortunately, cats often seem keen and able to adopt a kind of time-share arrangement with respect to their overlapping territories. However, as you might expect, the most dominant cats will retain the hunting rights in the best locations at the best times: this usually means at dawn and dusk.

Other cats with lower status have to fit in around them, and will take over the same territories when the more dominant cats have packed up and returned home. However, territorial disputes do take place, and some areas seem to stage more than their fair share of cat fights. Some cats also tend to get into more scraps

Cats are naturally territorial, and some will aggressively defend their patch. Such disputes may occur frequently in some neighbourhoods, but most cats prefer to avoid fighting.

during their lives than others. Fighting between cats can have the following consequences, both of which are potentially serious.

Injuries • Cat-bite wounds almost always become infected, and very often form painful swollen abscesses that require urgent medical attention and sometimes surgical treatment.

Transfer of infectious diseases • Very close contact between cats is a sure means of transferring the infectious organisms responsible for causing major diseases (see pages 118–20). In the UK, vaccines are available to help protect cats from most of the serious infectious diseases to which they may be exposed; one exception is feline immunodeficiency virus infection. The main route of transmission of this particular organism – which is related to the virus that causes human AIDS – is via the saliva injected from infected to uninfected cats through fight-induced bite wounds.

WARNING

If you live in an area in which many cats have access outdoors, where fights are common and where feline leukaemia virus and/or feline immunodeficiency virus infection are frequently diagnosed, you should consider keeping your kitten indoors from before dusk to after dawn. Ask at your vet centre for further information.

Leaving your kitten

There will be times when you have to leave your kitten. This may normally just be for a few hours, but there will also be times when you have to be away from him for longer periods, possibly at short notice.

Whether you are going away for a day or two, or for several weeks, you will need to make suitable arrangements for your kitten's care during that time. One option is to ask a friend or a relative to look after him. Alternatively, like most cat-owners, you could arrange for him to stay in a suitable cattery. And then, of course, there are kitten-sitters!

Leaving your kitten for short periods

Until you know that you can fully trust your kitten to behave himself indoors unsupervised, you should make sure that he is shut away safely in his playroom when you go out. If he is old enough, and able to go outdoors, you may choose to leave his cat flap open. If he is not free to venture outside, you must leave your kitten with at least one litter-tray (see page 75).

If you feed your kitten on moist food (see page 60) you should not leave him for more than the normal interval between meals, but if you feed him 'ad-lib' on dry food you can leave him for longer periods.

Initially, you are likely to be more anxious about leaving your kitten than he will be about being left. As he grows older, you will be able to leave him for longer times, with access to other parts of your house.

Leaving your kitten for longer periods

When you have to leave your kitten for more than a few hours – perhaps overnight or for several days or even weeks – you will need to arrange for someone else to care for him in your absence. The most obvious option is to board him at a suitable cattery.

CHOOSING A CATTERY

Even if you do not intend now to put your kitten into a cattery at any stage of his life, you never know how your circumstances may change. Sudden, unexpected work commitments or illness may mean that you need to board him at very short notice. Choose the boarding cattery that you would like to use well in advance, and – if possible – book early, as the best catteries often get booked up. Your kitten will need to be fully up-to-date with his main vaccinations (see pages 118–21).

Your kitten will appreciate the time and effort that you put into finding a really good cattery for him, and, what is more, you will be able to go away happy in the knowledge that he is in safe hands.

Where to start

• Look in telephone directories and local newspapers for advertisements of catteries, and also contact any national organizations that may recommend catteries. Make a list of all those within a reasonable distance from your home. However, do not think solely about their convenience: an extra 20 or 30 minutes' drive may perhaps put a much better cattery within reach.
• Draw up a shortlist of just a few catteries, based if possible on personal recommendations from your vet centre and from other cat-owners.

What to do next

• Ideally, you should then arrange to visit all of the catteries on your shortlist, as you will gain a much better feel for a place by seeing it. If the owners of an establishment say that they do not allow inspection visits, scrub them from your list.
• The owners of a good cattery should want to know all about your kitten, including his likes and dislikes, his diet, whether he has been in a cattery before and whether he has any special medical needs.
• At each cattery, ask to see its licence (this should be prominently displayed). When looking around, judge for yourself the conditions under which the guests are kept. It does not matter if the enclosures are fairly spartan, as you should be able to bring some of your kitten's own creature comforts, such as his bed. The enclosures should provide platforms on which cats may climb, as well as covered areas.

PREVENTING SEPARATION ANXIETY

Some cats do become anxious when their owners leave them. Just in case your kitten is one of them, you should 'cool off' your relationship with him in the few days prior to going away. Distance yourself from him emotionally, and give him less physical attention than normal.

Most cats adapt to life in boarding catteries very quickly. By booking your kitten into your chosen cattery for a few short stays early on during his life, you will be able to evaluate how he copes with the experience. You will also learn at first hand how well the staff at the cattery look after him.

• Check for 'sneeze-barriers'. These are 50-cm (20-in) gaps, or partitions, between enclosures, designed to prevent airborne transmission of any infectious organisms between adjacent occupants. Such barriers will also ensure that your kitten will not feel threatened by his neighbours. Check that the cattery has isolation facilities for sick cats, and find out what would happen if your kitten were unwell.
• Find out what the cattery would do if your return were delayed.
• Cats should be given free access to private exercise areas. If you see stacked cat cages in any cattery that you visit, turn around and leave.
• The property should be well-fenced with good fire-prevention measures. Someone should be on the premises 24 hours a day.
• Most important of all, value your first impressions about the cattery, and about its staff. Would you be happy to leave your kitten with them, and knowing him as well as you do, will he be happy to stay?

Items to take to the cattery

• An adequate supply of any special food items – if the cattery does not already stock them – and a clear and complete diet sheet for the staff to follow.
• Your kitten's vaccination card (see page 121), and contact details for your vet centre.
• Some of your kitten's own bedding, and a selection of his favourite toys.
• Your kitten's grooming equipment.
• Instructions as to what to do in an emergency, including your contact details while you are away.
• Precise instructions relating to any special medical or general-care procedures.

ALTERNATIVES TO A CATTERY

You could ask a friend to look after your kitten while you are away, but do not put anyone under pressure to do so. If you leave your kitten in your house and have someone coming in frequently to care for him, consider keeping him indoors while you are away. If you leave his cat flap open, he may disappear when his carer comes to visit, and he or she may never see him!

When you take your kitten to his cattery, make sure that you have all his belongings with you (see left), and try to avoid any long and lingering farewells.

Only allow another person to look after your kitten in his or her own home if he or she is an experienced cat-owner, has no other pets indoors and has a house that is safe and secure. It will be worth taking your kitten there for a 'trial' stay to see how he gets on. Under no circumstances should he be allowed outside while staying at another house. Personally, I would be very wary of agreeing to look after someone's kitten in my own house, as it would be a great responsibility.

KITTEN-SITTERS

Another option worth considering is that of employing someone to come and live in your house while you are away. If you have a number of other animals, this may also be the most cost-effective solution. Make sure that anyone whom you use gets on well with your kitten, has good references and is properly trained. Some kitten-sitters are very experienced and trustworthy.

Moving house with your kitten

If you are anything like most people, you will find moving house a very stressful event. Without your consideration and help, your kitten will probably not find it much fun either. If he stays at home during the packing, you may have to keep him shut away safely to prevent him from straying out through open doors. He will also sense that you are stressed, although his own state of mind will depend on his temperament and his ability to cope with new experiences.

How will your kitten react?

As all the hustle and bustle carries on around him, your kitten may become quiet and withdrawn, or he may become frantic. Whatever his reaction, he is likely to find all the unusual activity around the centre of his territory highly unsettling. There will be no logical reason, as far as he is concerned, that can explain why his territory is being systematically dismantled and removed by strangers.

Out of harm's way

If and when you move house, my advice would be to board your kitten with a suitable and willing friend, or preferably at a good cattery (see pages 94–5), from before the point at which you start to pack up your belongings right through until you are fairly settled in your new house. Cats also hate building work, so try to make sure that any alterations are complete by the time you bring him home from the cattery.

In this way your kitten will avoid all the disruption of the move itself, and you will be able to concentrate on the job in hand. You will also give yourself time to prepare the new house and garden for him, just as you did when he first arrived (see pages 50–1).

New house rules

You will have to answer many of the same questions with which you were faced when you were getting ready to bring your kitten home for the first time, and you may have to create some new house rules. Where will your kitten sleep? Which parts of the house will he be free to explore? What about access outdoors? Will moving house involve translocating his outdoor enclosure, or making the new garden kitten-proof?

When you bring your kitten to your new home, you will have to help him to settle in. He should be completely familiar with your new house before he has to cope with carving a niche for himself outdoors.

Finding a new vet centre

If you need to change your vet centre when you move house, you should make the arrangements in advance (see page 105) so that there is no period when your kitten is without a vet.

Bringing your kitten home

When you first bring your kitten back from the cattery or friend's house to your new home, you should treat him in the same way as you did when you brought him back from his breeder. Start by letting the kitten explore one safe room that you have designated as his playroom. Even though this will not be the same size and shape as his old one, it should contain many of its familiar sights and smells, including his bed, food and water bowls, litter-tray and scratching post.

Once you are sure that he is gaining confidence in his new surroundings, allow your kitten to explore – one at a time – all the other rooms to which he will eventually have free access in your new house. As in your old house, let him investigate his new territory at his own pace: simply supervise him and make sure that he cannot get out. This initial settling-in period may take just a few days, but with some sensitive cats it can go on for several weeks.

Venturing outdoors

If you plan to allow your kitten to go outdoors, his introduction to the world outside your new home should be as carefully orchestrated as it was in his former home. Before letting your kitten outdoors for the first time, do not feed him for 12 hours so that he is hungry. Avoid any time from dusk to dawn for this first excursion, as this will be when the most dominant

---

TAKING YOUR KITTEN ON HOLIDAY

Unless your kitten has a 'bomb-proof' disposition, loves travelling and has no interest in venturing away from his home base – wherever that may be – my advice is NOT to take him with you. You simply cannot tell how your kitten will react in unfamiliar surroundings and he could temporarily disappear, which would result in a miserable holiday for all of you. Far better options are to board him at a good cattery, or to leave him in the care of responsible friends (see pages 94–5).

cats in the neighbourhood will be on the prowl. Go with your kitten into the garden, but let him do a little exploring in his own time: just stand back and observe him quietly. Give him half an hour or so, and then call him indoors for something to eat. It is very important that your kitten quickly learns what his new home looks like from the outside, and also that he associates coming back through his new cat flap with the pleasant experience of a meal and your attention.

Repeat this 'short-burst' exposure outdoors on a number of occasions to reinforce the message. As your kitten becomes more and more confident, you can let him out for longer periods. Only let him out at night when he really is settled in and he knows the layout of your garden: then he can start to get to grips with evaluating the local cat population and organizing his territory time-share (see page 93).

Moving house within your kitten's territory

If your new house is close to your old one, it may be inside the limits of your kitten's existing territory (see pages 90–1). There is then the possibility that he will tread paths that lead back to his old house. The following steps should help to prevent him from gaining dual citizenship in both houses.

• Put in plenty of effort to make your kitten realize that he will get more care, love and attention in his new house than anywhere else.

• Make sure that the new owners of your old house are offhand with your kitten if he happens to turn up on their doorstep. If possible, his old cat flap should be locked.

• Ask any of your old neighbours to be equally dismissive of your kitten if he appears.

When you move house, it is a good idea to board your kitten at a cattery (or, failing this, with a friend), from before you start packing up right through until you are settled in and organized in your new home.

Responsible cat-ownership

The precise laws relating to cat-ownership may vary depending on where you live, but you can assume that, as a new cat-owner, you will have to obey some national laws and possibly other local ones.

Cat-ownership laws

In general, these laws aim to protect the welfare of all cats, and to ensure that cats are not a public or an environmental nuisance. All legal responsibilities apply to the person in charge of a cat at the time, and not just to his owner. Should an offence be committed, penalties such as fines, disqualification from owning a cat and even imprisonment may apply.

In the UK, there are no laws at the moment that relate specifically to the ownership of pet cats, but the welfare of cats is protected by laws that apply to all pet animals. To give you an idea, some of the main points currently in force are as follows.

• It is an offence to be cruel to a cat in any way. This means harming a cat either physically or mentally, including beating, kicking or terrifying him, carrying or transporting him in a way that causes suffering, or failing to provide him with adequate food and water. It also includes not taking any necessary action to prevent suffering, and failing to seek medical attention for a cat when required. It makes no difference at all whether the cruelty was intended or not: ignorance is no excuse, and is not considered so by law.

• It is an offence to abandon a cat – either temporarily or permanently – without reasonable cause or excuse. This rule includes letting a cat free to fend for himself as a stray, as well as keeping him shut away without due care and attention.

• The keeper of a cat may be liable for any damage that is caused by the cat either to other people or to their property.

YOUR KITTEN IS MISSING

Do not say that this could never happen to you – it could. I have known a number of people who have experienced the trauma of losing their cats, and all of them had thought that they were sufficiently diligent owners for it not to happen. Fortunately, many of these owners were – sooner or later – reunited with their cats, but others were not.

If you think that your kitten has strayed, or has not returned home in line with his normal routine, you must act quickly to try to find him.

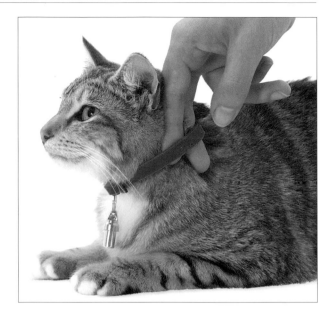

When fitting any kind of collar to your kitten, make sure that you can slip two fingers comfortably beneath the collar without having to stretch it.

Cats are generally keen to explore unfamiliar places. If you think your kitten is missing, he may have found his way inside your house to a place to which he does not normally have access. He may even be hiding in an unusual location, in which you would not think of looking for him. Alternatively, he may have wandered into another building nearby, such as your shed or garage, a neighbour's house or outbuildings, or even a local shop, office or school.

What to do first

If your kitten goes missing or does not return home as normal, the first steps to take are as follows.

• Look everywhere in your house for him. If you are doing some DIY on your home, you may have to check under the floorboards, or inside cavity walls or roof spaces. Call your kitten's name. If he eats a dry food, shaking some of the food in its container may help to attract his attention. Listen very carefully for the cry that he will make if he is within earshot but is trapped.

• If your kitten does not appear or you cannot find him indoors, go outside and continue to look, call, shake his food container and listen.

• If you are still unsuccessful in locating your kitten, visit as many local houses as you can to ask if anyone has seen him. Remember that – depending on his age, the number of other cats in your area and where you live – your kitten may have a territory of half a hectare or more. Ask neighbours to check inside their homes, sheds and other outbuildings. When they are open, search in all other local business and community premises.

identity tag   safety elastic

Your kitten's collar should incorporate a length of elastic. This will allow the collar to expand for safety, should it become snagged or caught in any way.

What to do next

If your investigations are fruitless and your kitten has still not returned within a further 12 hours, you should take the following actions.

• Notify every police station, animal-rescue centre, vet centre, cattery and pet shop over a very wide area surrounding the place in which you last saw your kitten. Provide them with a photograph as well as an accurate description of him (see below).

• If your kitten is permanently identified (see right), notify the national register that he is missing.

• Produce posters to put up in the local area, including public places such as vet centres, pet shops, libraries, petrol stations and pubs.

• Several times every day – especially at dawn and dusk – walk around your home and the local area, and try to attract your kitten's attention.

• Regularly visit in person the animal-rescue centres that you have already contacted.

• Even if you do not find your kitten quickly, do not give up. Owners are sometimes reunited with lost cats many months after their cats first went missing.

Identifying and registering your kitten

If you lose your kitten, you will stand a better chance of being reunited with him if you have permanently identified his body with a unique identity logged on to a national computer database. A precise description of him and details of his vital statistics will also be important (see below, left).

Even if it is not a legal responsibility where you live, my advice is that, if possible, you should identify your kitten with a microchip implant. Identity collars are not permanent, and may be lost or even removed during a kitten's outdoor activities. Alternatively, a tattoo – although an uncommon identification method for cats – may be an option in your area. Ask at your vet centre for details about all the identification and registration schemes in use where you live.

Implanting a microchip • A microchip is a very small device that is injected under a cat's skin, usually in his neck. Contrary to popular belief, this does not send out a constant electronic signal, but requires a piece of electronic equipment called a scanner to 'read' the unique identity with which the chip is programmed. This can only be done at short range. In my experience, implanting a microchip causes no greater discomfort to most cats than a routine vaccination. The advantage of a microchip is that it should be permanent; the disadvantages are that there is no way of telling – just by looking at a cat – whether he has a chip implanted, and no guarantee that the person who finds him will know to take him to someone with a scanner.

A tiny microchip is programmed with a unique identity that can be read by an instrument called a scanner. The microchip is injected under a cat's skin through a special needle.

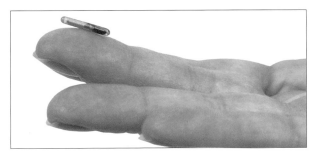

YOUR KITTEN'S DESCRIPTION

Whether or not you have your kitten permanently identified, you should still keep your own record of his appearance and vital statistics. Photograph him in good light from a number of angles. Draw a simple body map of him, and mark on it the location of any distinguishing features such as scars or markings that are impossible to see on a photograph. And what colour are his eyes?

These pictures and other details will help you to put together an accurate description of your kitten for circulation should he go missing. You will also be able to use them to create your own posters.

Health and hygiene

Keeping your kitten healthy does not simply mean taking him to his vet when he is unwell. You will need to implement a range of healthcare measures at home, including routine health-checks, grooming and parasite control. You must also take him to your vet centre for regular development checks and vaccinations.

Healthcare services

It is comforting to know that veterinary services are available 24 hours a day, 365 days a year from the majority of vet centres. Even those that do not provide out-of-hours services themselves should ensure that the needs of their patients are properly catered for in the event of an emergency.

VETERINARY PROFESSIONALS

The staff at your chosen vet centre will not only treat your kitten when he is unwell, but should also provide you with a range of services aimed at keeping him healthy. These preventive-medicine services include vaccination, parasite control, dental care and dietary advice. For the sake of your kitten, you should make good use of them.

A number of key people play a part in the day-to-day work of a typical vet centre. You will have more contact with some of them than with others, but all are an essential part of your kitten's veterinary team.

Receptionist

This is the first person whom you are likely to see at your vet centre. He or she will be responsible for booking appointments, handling enquiries, collecting fees and ensuring that clients are properly looked after. A dedicated receptionist should be adequately trained to offer general advice about animal healthcare.

Veterinary surgeons (Vets)

Although many vets specialize in the care of just one or two kinds of animal, every vet is trained to treat all creatures, great and small. The vet who looks after your kitten will not only be his physician but much more besides, including his personal surgeon, dentist, anaesthetist, pharmacist and even his psychiatrist.

Veterinary nurses

Veterinary nurses are highly trained and skilled, and are in my experience the backbone of many vet centres. Their responsibilities include running the operating theatre, assisting vets, caring for in-patients, running the dispensary, and carrying out laboratory tests. They may also undertake some minor surgical procedures.

Good vet centres will employ knowledgeable and caring staff, dedicated to providing their patients with the best of care.

| vet (centre owner) | head veterinary nurse | veterinary nurse | centre manager |

THE COSTS OF VETERINARY CARE

The vast majority of vet centres are run as private businesses, and you will have to pay for most of the services that you use. Health insurance is now an option for cat-owners who would like to budget for the unexpected costs of medical care (see page 105), and I would wholeheartedly recommend that you consider taking this out for your kitten.

Animal-care assistants

Unqualified, but nevertheless very caring, animal-care assistants are employed by some vet centres in order to reduce the workload of the nurses. These are often school-leavers or young people who may wish to gain some practical experience before going on to train as veterinary nurses. Feeding the in-patients, exercising them and cleaning up after them are all typical duties.

Other staff

Many larger vet centres also rely on the help of other staff, including a centre manager whose responsibility is the overall running of the centre and its finances. Additional staff will include cleaners and handymen. If your kitten ever has to stay in at your centre, he will no doubt get to know them – if only briefly.

receptionist   animal-care assistant   trainee veterinary nurse   vet (associate)

The layout of a typical vet centre

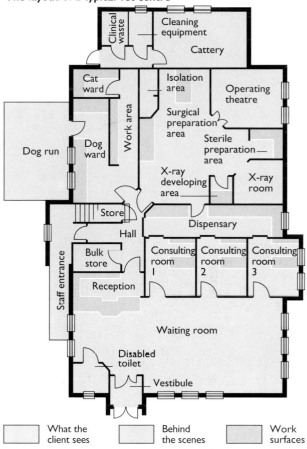

	What the client sees		Behind the scenes		Work surfaces

Most of the facilities at a vet centre are not on general view, but the staff should be happy to give you a guided tour.

TYPES OF VET CENTRE

There are a number of different types of vet centre. Some have the necessary facilities and staff to be able to treat animals of any sort; others concentrate solely on the care of pets.

The largest, best-equipped centres are sometimes known as veterinary hospitals. The smallest centres may be simple clinics with no surgical, diagnostic or in-patient facilities of their own, and are often part of a group of centres that includes a hospital.

More and more centres now run open days in order to allow existing and prospective clients to see behind the scenes (see page 104). To give you an idea of what to expect to see when you visit a vet centre, above is the interior plan of a typical centre with the facilities to treat both dog and cat patients.

VETERINARY SERVICES

The type, nature and range of services available from a particular vet centre will depend on the interests and expertise of the people who run it. Some vet centres may offer a comprehensive range of services aimed at cat- and dog-owners; others are more specialized (for instance, a centre may only take on cases referred to it by other centres). When choosing the vet centre that is best-suited to your kitten (see also pages 104–5), my advice would be to look for one that offers the types of services that are described here.

Accident-and-emergency care

In the UK, vet centres are required by law to provide clients with accident-and-emergency services 24 hours a day. Some centres may not do so themselves, but will arrange access to services provided by another centre in the area. Very few centres are actually open day and night for owners to arrive unannounced.

If you need veterinary help out of hours, you will normally have to telephone your vet centre. Answer accurately any questions relating to your kitten's symptoms, and listen carefully to any instructions you are given (it may be a good idea to write them down).

Depending on your kitten's symptoms, your vet may need to see him. A home visit may be essential in some cases, but – if possible – he or she will request that you take your kitten to the vet centre. With more facilities available there than your vet can bring in the back of the car, he or she will be able to examine and treat your kitten more easily and effectively.

Larger vet centres use sophisticated equipment to diagnose and treat a broad range of medical and surgical conditions of cats. This cat has been sedated for an X-ray investigation.

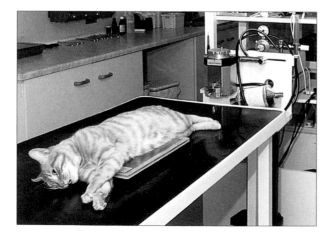

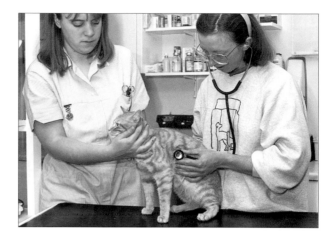

A normal consultation, conducted by your vet, should last for about 15 minutes. The vet may be assisted by a veterinary nurse, who may carry out your kitten's routine health-checks.

Consultations

During working hours, your vet centre should offer you the option of an individual consultation with your vet, during which he or she will examine your kitten if he is unwell or discuss any other health-related matter. Some centres also offer the option of a consultation with a veterinary nurse, for minor procedures or for advice on healthcare matters such as feeding.

The length of a consultation will vary, but it should last for at least 15 minutes. In my opinion, it is not possible to examine a cat, question his owner, make a diagnosis and decide on a treatment in less time than this. You should expect to pay a fixed fee for your kitten's appointment, plus extra for any tests, drugs or other products used. 'Open' surgeries are run on a first-come, first-seen basis; most vet centres organize surgeries several times a day.

Diagnostics

If your kitten is off-colour, your vet may decide to carry out some diagnostic tests to establish the cause of the problem. These may include straightforward procedures such as using a stethoscope, thermometer or ophthalmoscope (an instrument used to look at the eyes in detail). Alternatively, more complex procedures such as blood tests, radiology (taking X-ray pictures), recording an ECG (ElectroCardioGram: a test that measures electrical activity in the patient's heart), endoscopy (looking into body cavities using a long, thin camera) or an ultrasound scan may be necessary. Some diagnostic tests require the patient to be sedated or even anaesthetized. For these kinds of tests to be carried out, your kitten will probably be admitted to your vet centre as an in-patient.

Drugs dispensary

In most cases requiring therapy with drugs, treatment will begin at your vet centre during the consultation, but you will need to continue the administration of the drugs at home. Rather than giving out prescriptions, almost all vet centres run their own dispensaries to supply drugs. The dispensary is usually managed by a veterinary nurse, who will give you detailed advice about how to use any drugs prescribed.

Referrals

Very few vet centres will have all the necessary equipment and expertise to provide you with every veterinary and healthcare service that your kitten may require during his lifetime. If your kitten should at any time need some specialist treatment that is not available at your particular vet centre, your vet may suggest that you take him to see a vet who works at another centre (see page 105). If necessary, your vet should also be able to refer your kitten to other professionals involved in animal care, such as an animal-behaviour expert or even a physiotherapist.

Surgery

Dental descaling and polishing, castration and spaying, removing a broken nail, repairing a wound, mending a fractured bone and removing a growth or tumour are all considered surgical procedures.

All vet centres – apart from the smallest clinic-only centres – should have full surgical facilities. These will include anaesthetic equipment, an operating theatre stocked with instruments, and a post-anaesthetic recovery area. Some centres are also set up with specialist tools such as lasers and surgical freezing equipment, as well as other highly advanced items.

The complexity of the surgery that is undertaken at a particular centre will depend both upon the level of equipment and upon the expertise of the staff at that centre. Fees for surgery will comprise the cost of the anaesthetics used, the theatre time required and any additional items needed for the procedure, including cotton wool, syringes, needles and dressings.

If your kitten needs surgery of any kind, you must expect to receive a realistic bill from your vet centre. Remember that the technical skill that is required by a surgeon to carry out an operation will be the same whether the operation is on a human or a cat, and that often the equipment used is very similar.

Services for healthy cats

Your vet centre should offer you a range of products and services that will help you to keep your kitten healthy. For example, almost all vet centres will be able to vaccinate kittens (see pages 118–21).

Your centre should also stock a selection of healthcare products, including those designed for dental care and parasite control. A wide variety of specially formulated diets and other food items is now available from many centres.

Supplying you with products is only a part of ensuring good healthcare for your kitten. More important is the advice that you will need in order to select the most appropriate products and then to use them properly. Some veterinary nurses are specially trained to advise clients on all aspects of cat healthcare, including nutrition and behaviour. At many larger vet centres, nurses may be available to discuss these matters either on a one-to-one basis or in special group clinics.

In most good vet centres, veterinary nurses are on hand to offer advice on all aspects of pet care, and to carry out routine procedures such as weighing and development checks. Electronic weigh platforms such as this one – often used for larger animals – are now commonplace.

Choosing a vet centre

Recent research has shown that most people simply use the vet centre that is geographically nearest to their homes, but, as you will have discovered in the preceding pages, not all centres are the same. Your most convenient vet centre may turn out to be the one best-suited to your needs, but you should investigate the alternatives – if any exist – by following the step-by-step guide outlined here.

Try to make your initial decision about which vet centre you will use well before you even collect your kitten, so that you can benefit from all the advice and information that is available from the centre as you prepare to become a cat-owner.

What to do

1 Look in your local business telephone directory for addresses of vet centres, and then make a list of all those that are within 20 to 30 minutes' drive: this is really the furthest that you should need to travel in an emergency situation.

Speak to cat-owning friends to obtain their opinions of the centres on this initial list.

After completing their training, many vets go on to specialize in particular areas of veterinary science, such as orthopaedics or radiology (below). Your vet should be happy to refer your kitten to an appropriate expert if necessary.

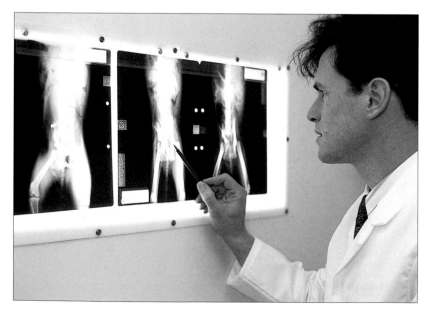

2 Create a shortlist of those centres with the facilities and expertise to treat cats.

3 Make a quick, unannounced visit to all the centres on your shortlist, and take note of each of the following aspects.
• The difficulty of the journey.
• The ease of access to the premises.
• The availability of parking facilities.
• The state of repair of the premises.
• The cleanliness of the waiting room and reception.
• The appearance and attitude of the reception staff.
• The manner in which other clients are handled.
While you are there, ask for information about all the services offered (see pages 102–3), the centre's opening times and the kinds of fees charged (many vet centres now produce proper brochures with this information). Find out whether it would be possible to arrange an appointment to have a tour of the centre's facilities.

4 Armed with all the information that you have obtained about each centre, and with the views of your friends in mind, prepare a new shortlist. Do not even consider a centre that is not prepared to give you a guided tour of their facilities: ask yourself what it must have to hide. All good vet centres should be happy to give you a guided tour, although this may have to be outside normal working hours for obvious reasons.

5 Having made the arrangements, go to view all the centres that you have shortlisted. If possible, take someone with you, as a second opinion is always valuable. While you are there, try to meet some of the veterinary staff. Take particular note of the following aspects.
• The overall cleanliness and state of repair of the facilities.
• The friendliness and professional attitude of the veterinary staff you meet during your tour.

6 Finally, go home, think carefully about everything that you have seen and heard at each centre, and then make your decision.

A SECOND OPINION

If your kitten is unwell and his condition does not seem to be improving despite treatment, your vet may decide that he should be examined by another vet for a second opinion. If this means taking your kitten to another vet centre, your vet should make the arrangements for you.

At any time, you may arrange a second opinion on your kitten's condition from another vet independently. However, some specialists will only take cases that are referred on to them by other vets.

Changing your vet

You may need to change your vet if you move house, and, if so, you should select a new vet centre in the same way as you did the first time (see opposite). When you register your kitten at the new vet centre, you will be asked by the receptionist for the name and address of your old centre so that your kitten's medical records can be transferred.

You may also wish to move to a new centre if you are unhappy with the service that either you or your kitten is receiving. However, before making a hasty decision do talk through any grievance that you have with an appropriate member of staff. It may be that the problem has occurred because of an unfortunate breakdown in communications somewhere along the line, and it would be a pity to leave a very good centre over what could be a simple misunderstanding.

HEALTH INSURANCE

The cost of any veterinary care that your kitten may require in his lifetime is the one item that is impossible for you to budget for. You can calculate the annual cost of some preventive healthcare procedures such as parasite control (see pages 114–17) and vaccination (see pages 118–21), but you cannot predict when your kitten will be ill, or when he may suffer an injury. And, if he does require veterinary treatment, there is no way of knowing in advance how sophisticated that treatment will need to be, or over what period of time your kitten may require it.

The cost of veterinary treatment is very good value for money compared with the cost of some equivalent medical treatments for humans, but an unexpected veterinary bill can make a substantial dent in your cashflow. Fortunately, however, it is now possible to insure animals against the cost of veterinary treatment, and many companies offer a range of policies to suit the needs of cat-owners.

For an annual premium, most insurance policies will guarantee to pay all your veterinary fees up to a maximum amount in each year. You will have to pay an agreed sum towards each claim (this is normally about 15 per cent). Some policies offer other kinds of cover as well. When choosing which policy to take out, make sure that you read all the small print and, if you are in any doubt, consult an insurance advisor.

I would very strongly recommend that you take out health insurance for your kitten. I find nothing worse than seeing an owner – already distraught about his or her cat's illness – coping with the extra worry of how to pay for his care.

A typical policy may cover the following aspects.
• Veterinary fees for illness and accidents, including physiotherapy, acupuncture, homoeopathic medicines, hospitalization and referral.
• Death following an accident or illness: the cost of your kitten will be reimbursed.
• Loss through theft or straying: the cost of your kitten will be reimbursed.
• Advertising and reward costs if your kitten is lost.
• Cattery fees for your cat, or home-care with a friend, if you are taken into hospital for more than four days.
• Holiday-cancellation costs if your kitten has surgery up to seven days before or while you are on holiday.

Unexpected veterinary fees can be an unwelcome burden. The chart below indicates the relative costs incurred in the first year of owning a pedigree kitten who suffers a serious injury.

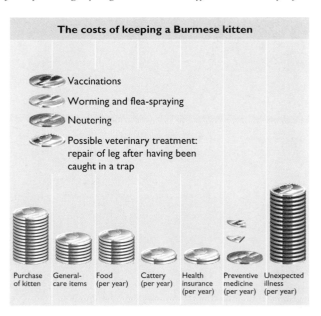

The costs of keeping a Burmese kitten

Vaccinations

Worming and flea-spraying

Neutering

Possible veterinary treatment: repair of leg after having been caught in a trap

Purchase of kitten | General-care items | Food (per year) | Cattery (per year) | Health insurance (per year) | Preventive medicine (per year) | Unexpected illness (per year)

Health-monitoring

You are an essential part of your kitten's healthcare team: in fact, you are the most important member of it. As his owner, it is you who have the ultimate responsibility for his diet, his mental and physical stimulation, and his day-to-day care. He will also rely on you to identify when he is unwell and to seek veterinary attention for him as and when necessary.

Why carry out health-checks?

Unfortunately, the signs and symptoms of many conditions may not be immediately obvious, so you should get into the habit early on of carrying out a simple health-check on your kitten at least once a week. By examining him thoroughly in this way, you are much more likely to pick up any health problems before they become crises.

Many cat-owners are unable to restrain their cats properly, and find it difficult if not impossible to carry out relatively straightforward tasks such as examining their cats' feet, or looking in their mouths. Often this is because their cats become aggressive and will not let

them do so. These cats are their own worst enemies, as their reluctance to be examined means that certain conditions go unnoticed by their owners. However, it is not their fault, as it is completely natural for a cat to be anxious about having his mouth examined or his paw inspected. However, such fears can easily be reduced, if not prevented entirely.

Restraining your kitten

By starting to carry out routine health-checks on your kitten from the time when he first comes to live with you, you will quickly help him to become familiar with the experience of being restrained and having the sensitive parts of his body examined. As he grows up, he will therefore see health-checks as routine and very normal events in his life. He may never relish the experience, but he should tolerate it.

With a little time and practice, you will become more efficient at restraining your kitten and carrying out health-checks, and, as a result, each session will be shorter and that much sweeter for both of you.

A basic health-check

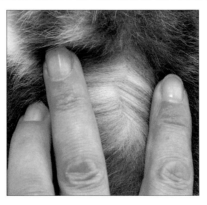

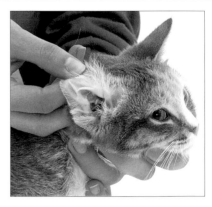

Mouth

Check for the following problems.
• Reddened, inflamed gum edges (see pages 112–13).
• Brown staining of the teeth, especially near the gums.
• Broken teeth.
• Unusually bad breath.
• Foreign bodies.

Hair and skin

Check for the following problems.
• Greasy hair or dandruff.
• Hair loss.
• Red, inflamed areas of skin.
• An abnormal smell to the coat.
• Foreign bodies.
• Fur mats (see page 109).
• Evidence of fleas (see page 117).

Ears

Check for the following problems.
• The presence of discharge at the ear holes.
• Dirt and debris at the ear holes.
• Reddened, inflamed ear holes or ear flaps.
• An abnormal smell at the ear holes.

Carrying out a health-check

When? • This is obviously up to you, but you will find health-checks easier if your kitten is sleepy rather than fired-up and hyperactive. You should weigh your kitten at the same time of day on each occasion, as natural variations in his body weight that occur during each 24-hour period could be misleading. A good time to carry out a health-check is while grooming your kitten (see pages 108–11).

Where? • Restraining your kitten for a physical examination will be simpler if he is off the ground on a suitable table (this should be covered with a non-slip mat). If he is a wriggler, ask an assistant to help you.

Who? • All the members of your family should carry out basic health-checks on your kitten. Not only are they a good way of bonding with him, but, if he is used to different people examining him, he will be much better-behaved when checked over by an unfamiliar person such as your vet.

WEIGHING YOUR KITTEN

You should be able to weigh your kitten in his carrying basket on a set of bathroom scales. Remember to deduct the weight of the basket!

However, while he is still very small your kitten may barely move the needle on a set of scales that is designed for people. In this case you could use a set of kitchen scales (see page 65), but you must ensure that the tray will not be used afterwards for food. Note down your kitten's weight whenever you weigh him.

What does a health-check involve?

There are certain important examinations that should be part of your health-check routine (see below, left), but the order in which you do them is up to you. One question is sure to keep cropping up: 'Is this normal?' What may at first sight appear to be an abnormality may just be a normal variation. For instance, you may be concerned about a black spot on your kitten's otherwise pink lips, but such markings are common. However, if such a mark suddenly appears, it may be more significant.

The more you examine your kitten, the better you will know his anatomical characteristics and the easier you will find it to recognize abnormalities. Use your eyes, nose and fingers to identify anything unusual in the way your kitten looks, feels or smells. Observe, too, how he reacts to being handled by you: any unusual resentment could indicate a painful spot.

Monitoring your kitten

In cats, behavioural changes are often early signs of disease. Over time, you will learn in detail what is normal behaviour for your kitten and will notice if he is acting oddly. You should also pay close attention to your kitten's sleep patterns, to his body waste, and to his food and water intake: sudden changes in any of these could be significant.

Feet

Check for the following problems.
• Overlong claws, especially the dew claws.
• Cracked or frayed claws.
• Cracked or damaged pads.
• Inflamed skin between the toes.
• Fur mats between the toes.
• Foreign bodies.

Eyes

Check for the following problems.
• Tear-stained fur around the eyes.
• Reddened inner eyelids.
• The third eyelids coming across the eyes.
• Cloudiness within the eyeballs.
• Dull surfaces to the eyes.
• Foreign bodies.

Grooming your kitten

Your kitten's skin is the largest of his body organs: the skin of an adult cat may cover over 0.25 square metre (1 sq ft). Strong but stretchy, your kitten's skin not only wraps and protects his skeleton, muscles and most other vital body structures, but also has many other important functions.

His skin allows him to experience touch, pressure, pain, itchiness, heat and cold, and stores a range of substances such as water, vitamins, fats, carbohydrates and proteins. However, perhaps the most obvious role of your kitten's skin is the production of his hair-coat, his nails and his foot pads.

Your kitten's hairy skin is a remarkable biological overcoat. It is the only one he has, and he will rely on you to help him to look after it. This is not simply to make him look attractive, but also to keep him healthy: skin disorders in cats are some of the most common medical problems presented to vets. By grooming your kitten on a regular basis, feeding him a high-quality, balanced diet and taking action to prevent infestations of skin parasites such as fleas (see pages 116–17), you will be doing all you can to make sure that his coat remains in top condition.

WHAT IS HAIR?

Hair is dead. It consists mostly of protein, and it is produced by special structures called follicles within the skin. A cat's diet will have a profound effect on the quantity and quality of his hair: inadequate nutrition may lead to a poor, brittle, dry or thin hair-coat.

Cats have three types of hair. Guard hairs are thick, straight and taper evenly to fine points; awn hairs are thinner and have small swellings near their tips; and down hairs – the thinnest type – are crimped or wavy.

Types of coat

The longest hairs of a short-coated cat are on average 4.5 cm (1¾ in) long, while a long-coated cat may have hairs over 12 cm (5 in) in length. In common with their ancestor, the African wild cat (see pages 8–9), most pet cats have short coats. All other kinds of coat have been created by man through artificially selecting cats with unusual coats to breed together.

Rex cats have curly hair (see page 47), and wire-haired cats have crimped coats. Those cats unfortunate enough to be born as members of the sphynx breed have virtually no coat at all – not even whiskers.

Grooming a long-haired kitten

1 Using a slicker brush, and starting at your kitten's feet, brush gently but firmly in stroking movements, reaching down to the depths of his coat. Then move on to the rest of his body, and finally groom his head, neck and chest.

2 Repeat the whole process using a metal comb to remove any loose hairs. If your kitten is one of the hairier individuals, you should pay particular attention to the areas of his beard, armpits, under his tail and down the backs of his legs.

3 Complete the grooming session by wiping away any discharge from the hair around your kitten's eyes and on the insides of his ear flaps. For this you can either use moist human face-wipes, or cotton wool dipped in clean water.

GROOMING EQUIPMENT

You will need a brush, a comb and some human face-wipes to groom your kitten. The range of equipment available is enormous: if your kitten has an unusual or long-haired coat, my advice is to ask a professional cat-groomer to recommend tools that he or she feels will be best-suited to that type of coat. A good groomer should also be happy to give you valuable tips on using the tools, especially if you book your kitten into his or her parlour every now and again for a full make-over!

Coat colours

Cats who have pale-coloured bodies and different-coloured extremities (noses, ear tips, paws and tail tips), such as the Siamese, have fur that changes colour depending on the outside temperature: the higher the temperature, the lighter their coat colour. This is why kittens of these breeds are light-coloured at birth, and why adult cats who are kept indoors in cold climates are paler than those who live outside.

The most common type of congenital deafness in cats is shown by those with white coats and blue eyes. Charles Darwin is reported to have said that all such cats are deaf, but this is untrue: a few do have normal hearing, and the deafness experienced by most white cats with blue eyes may not be complete.

Colouring and temperament

Some experts believe that a cat's coat colour may give an indication of his temperament. This subject is still being researched, but one study has revealed that cats with black, black-and-white or grey-tabby coats tend to have good personalities and are able to handle stress well. My own experience is that tortoiseshell cats can be fiery characters (all normal tortoiseshell cats are female).

Hair fact file

• A cat's hair lies in many different directions – called hair tracts – on different parts of his body. The hair normally slopes backwards along the body and downwards towards the feet. Doing so is thought to reduce 'drag' when the cat moves, and to encourage water to run off without soaking his skin.

• A cat's hair does not grow continuously, but in cycles. An individual hair will grow until it reaches a set length, governed by the cat's genes. It then stops growing, and may remain in place for several months before it is plucked out during grooming or rubbing, or is pushed out by another hair growing up from underneath. After a variable period (this depends on a number of factors including daylight length and ambient temperature), the hair will be shed.

• A cat does not go bald when he is shedding his coat, or moulting, because no two hairs near each other on his body are at the same part of the growth cycle at the same time.

• Most cats have periods of heavy coat replacement, or moulting, in the spring and summer. At these times, some cats may grow over 1 km (1½ miles) of hair per day. Some cats kept in conditions of artificial lighting and heating may moult all year round.

WHY GROOM YOUR KITTEN?

Although cats with different types of hair-coat need different kinds of coat care, all cats will benefit from regular and frequent grooming. A tangled, matted or dirty coat does not insulate a cat's body effectively, nor does it protect the underlying skin from damage. Without frequent and adequate grooming, a cat's hair-coat and the skin that produces it will be more vulnerable to disease.

A wild cat has to look after his own coat, and will use his tongue as a flannel and his teeth as a comb. Many pet cats look more glamorous than their wild relatives because they have quite unnatural but very

REMOVING A FUR MAT

A mat usually forms from loose hairs that have not been shed from the cat's coat and have become tangled. The cause is most often inadequate grooming. If you come across a mat when grooming your kitten, do not try to 'snatch' the brush or comb through it. You will not clear the mat and you will hurt your kitten.

To remove the mat, you will need a tool called a mat-breaker. Holding the base of the mat, work at it from the edge with the mat-breaker and it will gradually come apart. Finally, brush through the remaining hair using a slicker brush.

GROOMING A SHORT-HAIRED KITTEN

You may consider it unnecessary to groom your kitten if he has a short coat, but it will help to keep his coat in top condition. Generally, the most effective method is to start by grooming with a bristle brush to remove dirt and pull out any loose hairs. Starting with the least sensitive areas of his body, brush your kitten's entire coat thoroughly. Finish by combing him, and clean his eyes and ear flaps with face-wipes.

'fashionable' coats created through selective breeding. However, many of the more unusual kinds of hair-coat are prone to matting (see page 109) and are impossible for the cats to look after properly by themselves.

Cats of these breeds therefore need help in order to keep their coats in top condition, and will rely on their owners for grooming assistance.

When to groom

Some cats really enjoy being groomed, but many adults who have not been used to regular grooming from kittenhood resent it. For this reason, you should begin a daily grooming routine as soon as your kitten has settled in with you. You will find grooming easiest to carry out when he is fairly sleepy and relaxed: after a meal may be a good time.

At first, you should just groom your kitten on his back for a few minutes. Stop before he decides to walk off, so that you can spend some time just stroking him as a reward for remaining calm. Gradually increase the amount and extent of what you do to include the more sensitive parts of his body, such as under his tail and between his hindlegs. Try not to think of grooming as a chore: it is an important time for you and your kitten to bond with each other, as well as for you and other family members to practise your cat-handling skills.

The amount of time that you will need to spend grooming your kitten will depend on his coat type. Ideally, all cats should be thoroughly groomed once a week, and then given an additional quick tidy-up as and when necessary. You can carry out his routine health-checks (see pages 106–7) at the same time.

Where to groom

Always groom your kitten in the same place so that he becomes used to the routine. This should be a spot in which he is relaxed and will therefore be easier for you to handle. You may find that your lap is the best place, or you may find grooming simpler if your kitten is on a table covered with a non-slip mat.

Who should do the grooming?

Grooming your kitten is an excellent way of forming a good relationship with him, as well as practising some essential handling skills. For these reasons, all members of the household should be involved. Why not establish a grooming rota?

Cutting your kitten's claws

When you are at your vet centre, ask your vet or a veterinary nurse to show you the ideal length for your kitten's claws, and regularly check their length and condition yourself (see page 107). Never attempt to cut his claws without having watched a demonstration from your vet, a nurse or a professional cat-groomer.

GETTING EXPERT HELP

If your kitten has an unusual coat that requires special care, or he is particularly difficult and awkward to groom, you should seek specific coat-care advice from an experienced cat-groomer. If your kitten starts to scratch excessively, or his skin or coat looks abnormal in any way, do not hesitate to take him to your vet centre for a check-up. Skin conditions that may seem trivial at first can rapidly become more serious.

BATHING YOUR KITTEN

Only bath your kitten when absolutely necessary, as excessive bathing using shampoos may destroy the water-resistant qualities of his coat. In my experience, cats who smell usually have unhealthy skin that needs medical attention. A cat with very greasy or dry skin may also have a problem requiring specific treatment.

Few cats relish the experience of bathing, so you must be well-prepared, and you will need an assistant. Make sure that you use a shampoo that is pH balanced to a normal cat's skin – the range is 5.5 to 7.5 – for his body and a 'no-tears' baby shampoo for his face.

The best places to wash your kitten are in the bath or in a large washing-up bowl. Expect whatever room you do the bathing in to end up looking like the inside of a washing machine after a rinse cycle!

You will need

- A non-slip mat for the bottom of the bath (if using).
- An apron for yourself.
- Shampoo (and conditioner for a long-haired kitten).
- Plenty of towels.
- Cotton-wool plugs if your kitten has sensitive ears (remember to remove these afterwards).

With the help of an assistant, soak your kitten's coat with warm water from a jug before gently starting to shampoo it (dilute the shampoo with water to make rinsing easier).

After bathing your kitten, you should dry him as quickly as possible in order to prevent him from becoming chilled.

- Your well-brushed kitten, wearing his collar (your assistant will need to hold on to this, but beware that the dye used in some collars may run).

What to do

1 First of all, close the bathroom door. Do you want a soapy kitten running riot around your house, or worse, out through his cat flap? Dilute the shampoo. Test the water temperature, then lift your kitten into the bath or bowl, and wet his coat. Start at his feet and then work up his body, and finally soak his back (he is less likely to shake if you do it this way).

2 Shampoo your kitten's body, then gently wet and shampoo his head before rinsing him thoroughly. If you use a conditioner, follow its instructions.

3 Towel-dry your kitten, then finish him off with a hairdryer, brushing through his coat and keeping your hand in the airflow to ensure that you do not burn his skin. Do not blow-dry your kitten's face. Finally, comb him off and admire your handiwork.

Dental care

By far the most common oral disease of cats over two years old is periodontal, or gum, disease. You should be concerned about this even as the owner of a young kitten, because it is a long-term problem that starts in early life. It involves the build-up on the teeth of bacterial plaque, which – if it is left unhindered – may cause such extensive damage to the gums and supporting structures of the teeth that healthy teeth will either fall out or need to be extracted.

It may take months or even years for plaque to build up sufficiently to cause serious disease, but the problems start while a cat is still a young kitten. Some experts believe that more than eight out of 10 cats over two years old suffer from some degree of periodontal disease. However, in the early stages this condition is reversible, and this is why good, routine dental care for kittens from a young age is essential.

Teeth fact file

• Like humans, cats are not born with teeth.
• A kitten's first set of milk, or deciduous, teeth begins to erupt when he is between two and four weeks old. In all, he will have 26 milk teeth.
• When a kitten is around three months old, his milk teeth will be replaced by a set of permanent, adult teeth. These should all have erupted by the time the kitten is six months old.
• A cat's teeth are living structures that contain blood vessels and nerves, so they respond to pain.
• Cats have the fewest teeth of any of our common domestic mammals.
• Unlike those of a dog, a cat's teeth have no grinding surfaces. This is because cats are naturally adapted carnivores, and do not need to be able to grind down tough plant material. With the exception of crunching up dry food, cats do little – if any – chewing.
• Adult cats have four different types of teeth: incisors, canines, premolars and molars (there are no molar milk teeth in kittens).

Incisors • These are the small front teeth, used for cutting, nibbling, grooming and biting. When the mouth closes, the incisors in the upper jaw should come down just in front of those in the lower jaw.

Canines • These are the large 'eye-teeth', used for holding and tearing food items. They are also important in keeping a cat's tongue in his mouth and holding his lips in the correct position.

Premolars • These lie behind the canine teeth and are used for shearing, cutting and holding food.

Molars • These are at the back of the mouth.

PERIODONTAL DISEASE

The outer surface of a cat's teeth is made of enamel, the hardest material in his body. Day by day his teeth become covered in plaque, which consists mainly of bacteria. Through eating, this plaque is to some extent wiped from the smooth enamel of the teeth, but a little of it remains. Plaque is soft in texture, but it rapidly hardens to produce a substance called calculus, or tartar, which gradually thickens over time.

Without the benefit of regular tooth-brushing, many cats will suffer from a calculus build-up that – sooner or later – may be associated with severe periodontal disease.

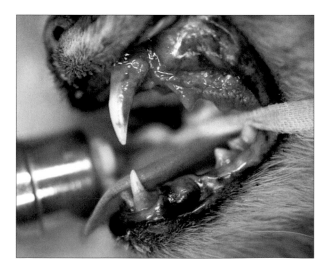

VISITING THE DENTIST

Your dental-care efforts at home are no guarantee that your kitten will not need some special dental care from time to time, although they should certainly curtail the frequency of such visits. Tooth-brushing will not remove hard calculus (tartar) and, if this forms on the teeth, it will need to be removed by your vet using an ultrasonic descaler. The procedure has to be carried out under a general anaesthetic and, once descaled and cleaned, the teeth are polished. Your kitten should have a thorough dental check-up by your vet at least once a year.

CATS AT RISK OF PERIODONTAL DISEASE

Some cats are more prone to periodontal disease than others. For example, breeds with fairly short, unnatural muzzles, such as the Peke-faced Persian (see page 44), have small mouths whose teeth are overcrowded.

This unusual alignment of the teeth allows food to become trapped, and bacterial plaque may be more difficult to remove from the teeth as a result. These types of cats tend to need more dental care than cats with naturally shaped faces.

Unlike enamel, calculus is rough, and so plaque is more difficult to remove from it. Bacteria in plaque near the gum edges irritate the gum – a condition called gingivitis – and, as the gum grows more and more inflamed, other damaging bacteria become involved. The gum may begin to recede around a tooth, and eventually the tooth becomes loose. The whole process can take several years to happen.

Prevention

The key to preventing periodontal disease is the regular removal of plaque before its presence causes damage. This can be done in the following ways.

Daily tooth-brushing • Regular brushing using the right toothpaste (see below, right) is a very effective way of removing bacterial plaque from teeth and disabling any small amounts left behind. It is an unusual and unnatural experience for a cat to have his teeth brushed, but it is a procedure to which most cats soon become accustomed, especially if familiarized with it from an early age.

Diet • The effects of different types of diet on the development of periodontal disease in cats is still under debate, but it may help to remove plaque and calculus if you offer your kitten small amounts of tough, fibrous meat such as heart, ox skirt, cheek muscle or bovine trachea to chew on once a week. Be very careful not to overdo this, however, or you may upset the overall balance of his diet.

BRUSHING YOUR KITTEN'S TEETH

Despite the fact that he will lose his milk teeth by the age of about six months (see opposite), you should start brushing your kitten's teeth as soon as you bring him home. As with so many procedures, the sooner he and you become used to tooth-brushing, the better. The best place to clean your kitten's teeth will be on a suitable table covered with a non-slip mat.

A special finger glove may be helpful in teaching your kitten to accept the experience of tooth-brushing. You should only begin to use an appropriate toothpaste (see below) once your kitten is happy to have his teeth brushed with water.

What to do

First let your kitten become accustomed to the feel of the toothbrush on his teeth and gums by holding back his lip and placing the brush in the pouch created by his cheek. Reward him for remaining calm.

Each day, increase the time that the brush stays in contact with your kitten's teeth and gums, and begin to move it about a little. Once your kitten is used to this experience, dip the brush in water, hold it with the head angled at 45 degrees towards the gum, and brush the teeth in circular movements. Before you start, ask at your vet centre for a tooth-brushing demonstration.

Tooth-brushing equipment

Toothbrush • You will need a brush with a very small head and firm bristles. Another option is a massage glove that fits over a finger (see above), although this may be less effective than a brush.

Toothpaste • Special toothpastes are made especially for pets. These are in many ways similar to human toothpastes, but they are more palatable to animals and do not foam.

Rinses and sprays • These solutions make a useful follow-up to brushing for those cats who seem to be particularly prone to gingivitis (see above, left).

Parasite prevention

Perhaps the best-known of all the parasites that live inside cats are tapeworms and roundworms, while in many countries fleas are their most common external parasites. Both worms and fleas can cause disease in cats, and they can also affect people.

What are parasites?

Parasites are organisms that live in or on other animals and derive their nourishment from them. Like humans and many other creatures, cats are covered with and contain numerous different types of parasite. In fact, they are walking zoos!

Some parasites are microscopic, while others can be seen by the naked eye. Not all parasites are harmful: for instance, a cat's skin and the lining of his airway and lungs are home to a number of bacteria that cause no problems under normal circumstances, although they may make him unwell if these tissues become damaged in any way.

TAPEWORMS

Perhaps the most common tapeworm to affect cats in the UK is *Dipylidium caninum*. Adult tapeworms live in a cat's small intestine. They are flat and white, and consist of many small segments.

TAENIA TAENIAEFORMIS WORMS

These worms are more substantial than *Dipylidium caninum* tapeworms. Normally only three or four will be present in an infested cat's intestines at the same time, but each may be up to 30 cm (12 in) long.

Instead of being eaten by fleas or lice, eggs from these tapeworms need to be eaten by small rodents – such as rats and mice – to continue their development. As a result, this kind of tapeworm is normally only a problem in cats who are habitual hunters.

How does a cat become infested?

Segments of an adult tapeworm, containing eggs, break off inside a cat's intestines and leave his body in his faeces. These segments then release their eggs. A flea larva (or a louse) in the environment may eat the eggs, which continue to develop inside the flea.

As an adult, the flea will search for an animal to jump aboard to suck blood: this may be the same cat, another cat, a dog or even a person. The animal may then swallow the flea during his grooming activities. The flea will be digested and will release immature tapeworms into the animal's intestines, where they go on to develop into adults – and so the cycle continues.

What are the signs of infestation?

There may be no signs at all if only a few tapeworms are present, or segments may be visible on the fur around the cat's anus or on the ground. A heavy infestation may cause digestive disturbances and anal irritation.

Are kittens vulnerable?

If there are fleas in his environment carrying immature tapeworms, your kitten may become infested.

It takes three weeks from the time when a flea is swallowed until the adult tapeworm produces more eggs. The earliest that you would see any signs is therefore when

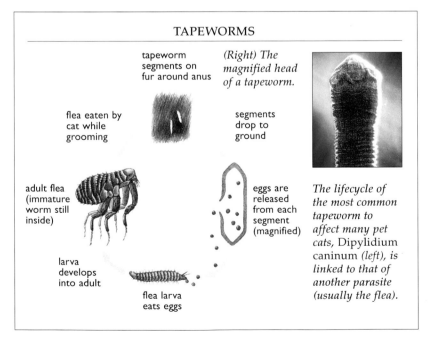

TAPEWORMS

tapeworm segments on fur around anus

(Right) The magnified head of a tapeworm.

flea eaten by cat while grooming

segments drop to ground

adult flea (immature worm still inside)

eggs are released from each segment (magnified)

larva develops into adult

flea larva eats eggs

The lifecycle of the most common tapeworm to affect many pet cats, Dipylidium caninum (left), is linked to that of another parasite (usually the flea).

your kitten has been with you for a few weeks (unless he came to you already infested).

Can tapeworms affect people?

A person may become infested by swallowing a tapeworm-carrying flea concealed in a cat's fur.

What should you do?

• Adopt a prevention campaign using a wormer recommended by your vet. Begin dosing your kitten as soon as he comes to live with you, and continue to do so at the appropriate intervals: I recommend all my clients to worm their kittens and cats against tapeworms every two to three months. Wormers can be given by mouth or by injection.
• Your campaign should include thorough flea control (see page 117).

ROUNDWORMS

There are numerous types of roundworm, including ascarids, hookworms, heartworms and lungworms. Perhaps the most significant roundworm in the UK is an ascarid called *Toxocara cati*. Adult roundworms of this type may grow up to 15 cm (6 in) in length. They live in the small intestine of an infested kitten, and in other tissues in an infested adult cat.

How does a cat become infested?

Your kitten may become infested with *Toxocara cati* roundworms in the following three ways.
Directly from his mother's milk • Most kittens are first infested in this way. Immature roundworms that have developed from eggs recently eaten by a queen, or that have been lying dormant in other tissues in her body, will appear in her milk during lactation. These will be swallowed by her kittens as they drink. The immature worms then develop into adult roundworms in the kittens' intestines, where they will produce more eggs. An adult female roundworm is capable of producing as many as 250,000 eggs in a single day.
By ingesting worm eggs in the environment • Eggs passed out in an infested cat's faeces take many weeks to develop to a stage at which they can

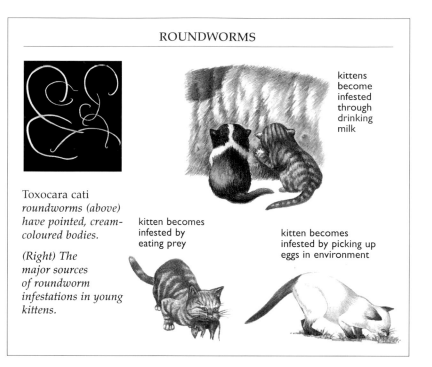

ROUNDWORMS

Toxocara cati roundworms (above) have pointed, cream-coloured bodies.

(Right) The major sources of roundworm infestations in young kittens.

kittens become infested through drinking milk

kitten becomes infested by eating prey

kitten becomes infested by picking up eggs in environment

infest another cat. However, once the eggs have reached that stage and are swallowed by a kitten, larvae hatch out of the eggs and will continue their development inside the kitten's body. After about six weeks, the larvae develop into adults in the intestines. In adult cats, the larvae travel through the intestinal wall and then become dormant in other tissues (adult roundworms are not normally found in the intestines of adult cats).
By eating other infested animals • If roundworm eggs capable of infesting another cat are eaten by an earthworm, beetle, rodent or bird, the immature worms will hatch out, find their way into the body tissues of their host and then become dormant. Through his natural hunting behaviour, a kitten may become infested with these worms by eating the carrier's body. The immature worms will be released during the process of digestion and will develop into egg-laying adults.

What are the signs of infestation?

Often there are no signs, although a heavy roundworm infestation in a kitten who is less than eight weeks old may cause digestive upsets. Adult roundworms are occasionally vomited by an infested kitten, or may be passed as a tangled knot of dead and dying worms in his faeces. Roundworm eggs are microscopic.

Can roundworms affect people?

People may unwittingly pick up eggs on their hands from the environment and – especially in the case of children – may transfer them from their hands or other contaminated objects into their mouths.

Once inside a person's intestines, the eggs will hatch and the immature worms may cause damage and disease as they move around the body. However, medical problems in people, caused by *Toxocara cati*, are thought to be extremely rare.

The following are important ways of reducing the risks of infestation even further.
• Ensure that children always wash their hands before eating, and firmly discourage them from 'mouthing' objects that have been in contact with soil.
• Cover food to prevent contamination by flies.
• Clear up your kitten's faeces as soon as possible.

What should you do?

If he has not been wormed by his breeder, your kitten will almost certainly have roundworms present in his intestines when you collect him. Even if his breeder has wormed him, you should still adopt a prevention campaign right away, using a wormer recommended by your vet. The timing and method of worming will depend on the product used, but your prevention campaign should include the following elements.
• Regularly treat your kitten with a recommended wormer, at appropriate intervals. A common regime is to worm kittens at two weeks old, and then every two weeks until they are 12 weeks old. Most vets will recommend worming kittens over this age (and adult cats) every three months. Wormers are available in liquid, tablet or powder form, and are administered by mouth. Some products are effective against both tapeworms and roundworms.
• Promptly remove and dispose of faeces from your kitten's litter-trays or other sites such as your garden, to prevent the development of roundworm eggs.

OTHER TYPES OF WORM

Depending on where you live and your kitten's lifestyle, he may be vulnerable to infestation with additional types of worm. Heartworm, for example, is prevalent in some parts of the USA.

You should check on this, and on any preventive measures that you should take, by asking at your vet centre about the worm situation in your area.

FLEAS

Cats may become infested by a number of insects and other creatures, including lice, ticks and different kinds of mite, but by far the most common external parasites to infest cats in many countries are fleas.

Fleas are wingless insects measuring less than 3 mm (⅛ in). They are quite remarkable little creatures: an adult can jump as many as 600 times an hour, and each jump is the equivalent of a person clearing a 50-storey skyscraper in one leap. There are about 3000 different types of flea, of which the one most commonly found on cats – and dogs – is the cat flea.

The lifecycle of the flea

life-sized flea

adult flea on cat

cocoon

eggs drop from cat's coat into environment

larva hatches from each egg

In one form or another, fleas spend most of their lives in the environment, only jumping on to a warmblooded animal – such as a cat – in order to feed and breed.

How does a cat become infested?

Fleas live in the environment: to them, cats and other warmblooded animals such as dogs and even people are simply roving restaurants. Adult fleas will jump on to a passing cat to feed, hanging on to his fur with their claws and biting through his skin to suck blood using their needle-like mouthparts. While they are on the cat, the fleas frantically mate. The females lay hundreds of eggs, which will generally drop from the cat's coat to the ground within eight hours.

In under two weeks a flea larva hatches from each egg, and hides in a dark place such as in bedding or upholstery. There it feeds on adult flea droppings and food crumbs, together with flakes of skin – and, of course, tapeworm eggs (see page 114).

When it is about 6 mm (¼ in) long, the larva spins itself a cocoon and completely digests itself – brain, nervous system, guts and all – before building an adult body. As an adult, it can survive for up to eight months waiting for a cat or dog meal to come along. When it senses vibration, it begins to jump.

Your kitten may pick up fleas from any of the following sources.
• Directly from another cat.
• Directly from a dog.
• Directly from another animal, such as a rabbit.
• From the environment in which the above animals live, or which they visit.

The reproductive ability of fleas is remarkable. If your kitten comes in one day with just 10 fleas on his coat, within four weeks there could be over 250,000 of them living in your house.

What are the signs of infestation?

In your house • Fleas are so common that almost all houses that contain pets – and many that do not – have a resident population. Fleas are visible to the naked eye, but they are very fast-moving so it is unusual to spot them in the environment.

On your kitten • Some cats are very sensitive to fleas and, even with only a very low infestation in their environment, may show marked signs of irritation, including excessive scratching, licking and fur-nibbling. There may also be tiny raised, red lumps on their skin. However, other cats may show little or no reaction at all to fleas.

On you • Remember that – if a hungry flea cannot find a cat or a dog – it may leap on to you to feed. Having sucked some blood, it will jump off again and resume its wait for a cat or a dog. You will be well aware of the presence of fleas in your house if you are sensitive to them.

What should you do?

Remember that fleas live most of their lives in the environment, not on cats. You must adopt a thorough prevention campaign, not only because you may not want fleas in your house, but also because they are a common cause of skin problems in cats and the main source of tapeworm infestation (see pages 114–15).

TESTING YOUR KITTEN FOR FLEAS

A telltale sign that fleas have been feeding on your kitten is the presence of tiny black specks in his coat. These flea droppings are relatively easy to identify if you sit your kitten on a white sheet of paper and brush any debris in his coat on to it. Dab up any specks that look suspicious with damp cotton wool: if the specks are flea droppings, they will dissolve and produce reddish-brown stains of partly digested blood.

WARNING

Insecticides are dangerous chemicals – they need to be in order to work – so always handle them with respect and follow their instructions very carefully. Do not use more than one product at one time, and never use sprays that are intended for the control of fleas in the environment on your kitten.

You should implement the following measures.
• Regularly vacuum-clean and then wash all your kitten's bedding.
• Regularly vacuum-clean your house.
• Regularly spray your house with an insecticide that is designed to kill adult fleas. The best products will also prevent flea eggs from developing.
• Regularly treat your kitten with insecticidal products made for cats. These are available as sprays, powders, foams, drops and shampoos for external use, as well as preparations to administer by mouth. Insecticidal collars are also an option.

When spraying against fleas, your kitten should be in an unfamiliar place – such as on a table top – and properly restrained by the scruff. If you are unsure of what to do, ask your vet or a veterinary nurse for a demonstration.

Vaccination

All kittens are vulnerable to diseases caused by microscopic living organisms – such as certain viruses – that may be rapidly passed on from one infected cat to others. Usually referred to as the major infectious diseases of cats, these include so-called 'cat 'flu', feline leukaemia virus infection and rabies.

The likelihood of your kitten encountering the organisms that cause any of these major infectious diseases will depend on his lifestyle: if he regularly visits places frequented by other cats, his chances of encountering the organisms will obviously be higher than if he is confined indoors.

The role of the immune system

If a cat becomes infected by a particular organism, his immune system should react to try to destroy it. However, the organisms that cause many of the major infectious diseases are so quick to damage vital body organs and structures that the cat's immune system may not be able to respond sufficiently quickly.

What does vaccination do?

Vaccination improves the speed and effectiveness of a cat's immune response to infection. It does this by stimulating the immune system through exposure to harmless quantities of the organism concerned, before the cat encounters that organism for real.

Protecting your kitten

To help protect your kitten from the major infectious diseases, you must ensure that he has completed a primary-vaccination course by the age of 12 weeks, and that he is given booster vaccinations every year (see pages 120–1).

Remember that failure to keep up with your kitten's vaccinations may put his life at risk.

Vaccines are generally injected under a cat's skin, normally over the neck. Such injections should only feel like a small scratch, and are accepted by most cats without fuss.

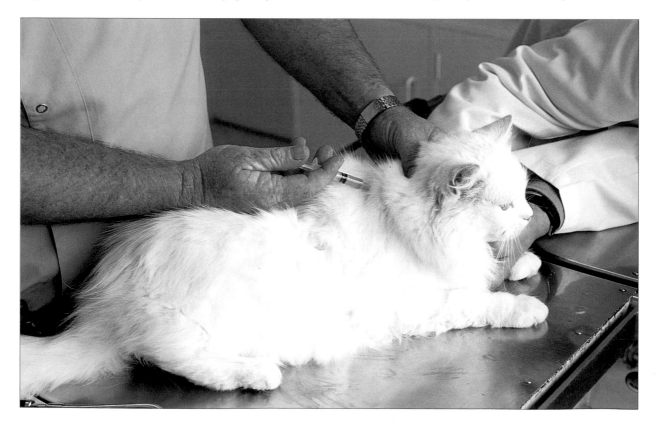

THE MAJOR INFECTIOUS DISEASES

The specific infectious diseases to which your kitten may be exposed will depend on where you live and on his lifestyle. These factors will therefore affect his vaccination requirements. You must discuss your kitten's vaccination needs with your vet.

Some of the most common infectious diseases – against which most vets will recommend routinely vaccinating cats – are described below and overleaf.

Feline panleucopenia (Viral enteritis)

This worldwide disease was the first viral disease of the cat ever discovered. It is a very tough virus and can survive outside a cat's body for up to one year.

What causes it? • A cat may become infected through close contact with another infected cat, or through being exposed to the virus in the environment. Once taken in through the mouth or nose, the virus will damage a number of tissues, including a cat's intestines and bone marrow.

Symptoms • The symptoms of this disease will vary depending on the severity of infection, but they usually include fever, vomiting, diarrhoea, lethargy and anorexia. In some affected cats this disease is characterized by little more than a fever; other cats are simply found dead. The disease is most severe in young kittens.

Treatment • There is no specific treatment available for feline panleucopenia.

Feline upper-respiratory-tract disease

Most commonly caused by one of two viruses – feline calicivirus or feline herpesvirus 1 – this disease is best-known as 'cat 'flu', and is most common in situations in which a number of cats are kept together, such as in boarding catteries and breeding colonies.

What causes it? • A cat will usually become infected through direct contact with another cat suffering from 'cat 'flu', although an apparently healthy cat who has had the disease in the past may still carry the virus and pass it on. Both viruses will survive for a short time in the environment.

Symptoms • Feline herpesvirus 1 usually causes more severe symptoms than feline calicivirus, but both may cause depression, sneezing, inappetence, fever, eye and nasal discharges, and tongue ulcers. 'Cat 'flu' is a distressing disease, but few cats die of it: those who do so are usually young kittens or older animals with incompetent immune systems.

Treatment • This involves the use of antibiotics to prevent secondary bacterial infections.

IMPORTANT NOTE

Two other major infectious diseases, against which there are currently no vaccinations in the UK, are the following (speak to your vet for further information).

• Feline immunodeficiency virus infection (see page 93).

• Feline coronavirus infection (Infectious peritonitis).

OTHER INFECTIOUS DISEASES

The following are additional major infectious diseases of cats, against which there are vaccinations available. Vaccination policies relating to these diseases vary, so ask at your vet centre for specific advice concerning any vaccinations that your kitten should be given in addition to those routinely recommended.

Feline leukaemia virus infection

This is a very complex disease. It is currently causing great concern among owners, and is therefore worth examining in detail. Some 30 years on from its initial discovery in 1964, this microscopic menace is now considered by many veterinary experts in the UK to be one of the most significant causes of feline disease.

Feline leukaemia virus infection belongs to a group of viruses known as 'retroviruses'. Other members of this group include viruses that can affect animals including sheep, cattle, horses and man. Human immunodeficiency virus (HIV), the cause of human AIDS, is probably the best-known retrovirus, but – make no mistake – feline leukaemia virus infection is not the cat equivalent of human AIDS. The virus has been found in every country tested for it, and is highly infectious. In the UK, up to one in 20 healthy cats may be infected.

What causes it? • The virus is present in the saliva, urine, blood, milk, respiratory mucus and faeces of permanently infected cats. Saliva is the most common source of infection to other cats, and the virus can be passed on by the close contact involved in licking and biting. Contaminated food bowls are also a source of infection. However, it usually takes much more than one lick for a cat to become infected. Kittens can also pick up feline leukaemia virus infection from their mothers, either before birth via their own placentas or after birth through drinking their milk.

Symptoms • There are no characteristic signs of feline leukaemia virus infection. A cat who is fighting the initial infection may simply appear off-colour, and in most cases the original infection probably goes unnoticed. Many of the signs of more advanced disease are also rather non-specific. As one of the main effects of permanent feline leukaemia virus infection is a 'damping down' of the cat's immune system, the actual symptoms are often those of other infections to which this disease has made the cat prone. The most common suspicious signs of permanent infection include weight loss, fever, anaemia, mouth ulcers, gum disease, swollen glands, diarrhoea, vomiting and conjunctivitis. However, these signs may occur months or even years after initial infection. A permanently infected cat may appear to be completely healthy during the incubation period, yet all the time he is pumping out the virus and constitutes a serious health risk to other cats with whom he comes into contact.

What is the prognosis? • The majority of cats will come into close contact with the feline leukaemia virus at least once in their lives, but only seven out of every 10 cats exposed to it will actually become infected. If a cat does become infected by the virus, there are three possible outcomes.

• The cat may successfully fight off the infection, and will become naturally immune to re-infection. This is generally the rule in older cats.

• The cat may be overwhelmed by the virus. His immune system may not be able to cope, and his body will be permanently infected. He will then become a virus 'factory', making the virus particles and then exporting them to the outside world from within his body. In general, this is the expected result in around three out of every 10 cats exposed to the virus, and is the norm in infections of unborn kittens and those less than eight weeks old.

• The cat's immune system may mount an attack on the virus but not beat it off completely. In this case, some virus will remain inside his body. Given enough time, some affected cats will manage to get rid of their infection; others do not.

Treatment • No drugs are available with which to treat feline leukaemia virus infection. The majority of permanently infected cats die within three-and-a-half years of being infected.

Prevention • Your vet centre may have a policy of recommending that all kittens are blood-tested prior to vaccination against feline leukaemia virus infection, in order to identify whether or not they are already infected with the virus. You should discuss this question in greater detail with your vet or a veterinary nurse.

Feline chlamydial infection

Chlamydia are very specialized bacteria. One type is considered a fairly common cause of conjunctivitis in cats, and may complicate 'cat 'flu' in some cases. Feline chlamydial infection is most frequently found in kittens of between five weeks and nine months old.

What causes it? • A cat may become infected through close contact with the eye or nasal discharges of other infected individuals, or via direct contact with a cat who has recovered from the disease but is still infected with the organisms.

Symptoms • Weeping, reddened eyes and swollen eyelids are the most obvious symptoms. A cat suffering from chlamydial infection may also have a mild nasal discharge and may sneeze. In most cases, cats are generally well and continue to eat.

Treatment • Chlamydia are susceptible to certain antibiotics. A vaccine against feline chlamydial infection exists in the UK, but is normally only administered to cats who are considered to be at particular risk of infection: for example, kittens going to live with other cats who have recently recovered from infection.

WHEN TO VACCINATE

The precise timing of your kitten's vaccinations will depend both on the products used and on the current veterinary recommendations about vaccination in your region or country. Your vet centre will advise you on when your kitten should be vaccinated.

Natural protection

For the first few weeks of your kitten's life, while his own immune system is developing, he should be protected from the major infectious diseases of cats by consuming antibodies in his mother's first milk, or colostrum. The protection that he obtains from these so-called maternal antibodies will wane as your kitten grows older, and will normally have disappeared by the time he is 12 weeks old.

Your kitten's vaccination regime

Expect your kitten's first vaccination course to consist of two vaccination sessions, several weeks apart. In the UK, a typical vaccination regime may be as follows.

At nine weeks • Vaccination against feline calicivirus and feline herpesvirus 1 (the viruses responsible for feline upper-respiratory-tract disease), and feline leukaemia virus. The three vaccinations may all be administered together as one injection under the skin, or the vaccination against feline leukaemia virus infection may be given separately.

At 12 weeks • A repeat of the vaccinations given at nine weeks. A kitten should not be allowed to go outdoors, or be introduced to other cats (other than those with whom he lives), until seven to 10 days after this second set of vaccinations.

At 15 months • A repeat of the vaccinations given at nine and 12 weeks. From this point onwards, the same vaccinations are given at 12-monthly intervals, and are usually referred to as boosters. Your vet centre will probably send your kitten a reminder when he is due to be vaccinated. It may well be the only post he ever gets!

Vaccinating your kitten on a routine and regular basis is an essential part of preventive healthcare. Make sure that you budget each year for vaccination costs, and never be tempted to omit having vaccinations carried out as a cost-cutting measure. The price that you end up paying could be your kitten's life.

By following the recommended vaccination programme in your area or country, you will be doing all you can to protect your kitten from the major infectious diseases.

NOTES ON VACCINATION

• Your vet or veterinary nurse should give you a record card containing details of the vaccinations administered to your kitten. Keep this in a safe place with his other medical records, and expect to be asked to produce it when you book him into a boarding cattery or at any time by your vet.

• Obvious reactions to vaccinations are unusual, but some kittens may be a little quieter than normal for about 24 hours after vaccination. However, if you think that your kitten has reacted badly to a vaccination, contact your vet centre immediately.

• Vaccinations are not guaranteed to protect your kitten from all the infectious diseases with which he may come into contact, as there will always be a small number of cats who do not respond fully to vaccination. There are also some diseases against which vaccinations are as yet unavailable (see page 119). However, by arranging for your kitten to have all the relevant vaccinations at the appropriate times, you will help to ensure that he does not suffer from a major infectious disease that could perhaps have been avoided.

Family planning

Well before your kitten reaches puberty, you must consider whether or not you would like him or her to parent a litter of kittens in the future. This is not a decision to be taken lightly. Cat-breeding brings serious responsibilities, and animal-rescue centres are full of unwanted young cats.

If after careful consideration you decide that you would like to breed from your cat, speak to your vet centre before making any arrangements. If, however, you have no desire to hear the patter of tiny furry feet, you should decide on a permanent method of birth control before your kitten is six months old.

The onset of puberty

In a non-pedigree cat, this is thought to be associated with body weight. Queens first come into heat when they reach 2.3–2.5 kg (5–5½ lb) at about seven months of age. Puberty occurs in toms when they are a month or two older, and about 1 kg (2¼ lb) heavier.

The onset of sexual activity is much more variable in pedigree cats. For instance, Siamese and Burmese queens may have their first heats when they are just five months old, whereas pedigree long-haired queens may not reach puberty in their first year.

The onset of sexual activity in a female kitten will also depend on the time of year when she was born. A female born in early spring may reach puberty in autumn that year, while a female born later in the year may not come into heat until the following spring.

TOM CATS

Having reached sexual maturity, male cats will be sexually active for the same periods of the year as queens. Those who are allowed to go outdoors will find mates and become fathers during the breeding season. The only way to prevent a free-roaming tom cat from becoming a father is to castrate him.

Castration

Castration is a surgical operation to neuter a male animal, carried out under a general anaesthetic. The base of the scrotum is opened and the testicles are removed, leaving small wounds that usually heal in about a week. Most cats do not suffer any lasting ill-effects, although castrated kittens do not develop the solid, muscular build that is characteristic of tom cats.

Tom cats are routinely castrated in the UK at six months of age (or younger if they live with unneutered females). Castrated tom cats can remain fertile for up to one month after being castrated.

Advantages
• Castrated males cannot father unwanted kittens.
• They tend not to wander as far from home.
• They are less likely to urine-mark indoor territories.
• Castration sets the example that birth control is not just the responsibility of owners of female cats.
• It reduces frustration and the desire to escape among male cats kept entirely indoors, or whose movements outdoors are restricted by their owners.

The reproductive anatomy of a tom cat

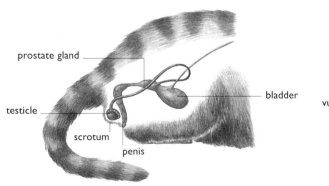

prostate gland

testicle

scrotum

penis

bladder

A healthy male (tom) cat, has two testicles that lie in a skin sac called the scrotum.

The reproductive anatomy of a queen

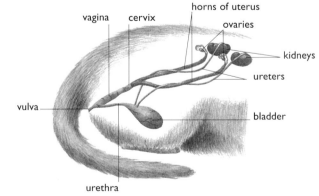

vagina   cervix   horns of uterus

ovaries

vulva

kidneys

ureters

bladder

urethra

A queen has two ovaries, one of which is near each of her kidneys. The uterus is Y-shaped.

QUEENS

Mature queens are not normally capable of becoming pregnant all year round, and are only sexually active during a breeding season that is switched on and off by changes in daylight hours. If kept in artificial lighting conditions, a queen will be sexually active all year round.

The queen in heat

At the onset of the breeding season, a queen will come into heat. This is a period of four to 10 days when she is receptive to the sexual advances of tom cats. She will become very vocal, and will rub and roll on the ground to attract the attention of males (see page 12).

Some unmated, non-pedigree queens come into heat every three

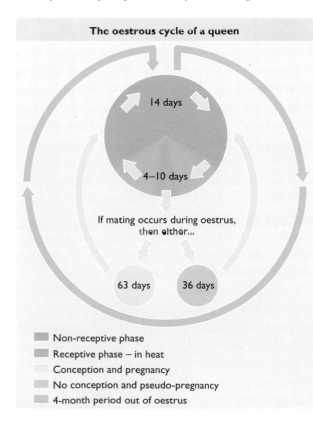

If you plan to breed from a female kitten, you must wait until she is mature and experiencing normal oestrous cycles. Discuss your plans with your vet well in advance.

The oestrous cycle (below) denotes the events that occur from the onset of one heat to a queen's next heat. Most queens are sexually inactive for a four-month period during the winter.

The oestrous cycle of a queen

14 days

4–10 days

If mating occurs during oestrus, then either...

63 days

36 days

■ Non-receptive phase
■ Receptive phase – in heat
■ Conception and pregnancy
■ No conception and pseudo-pregnancy
■ 4-month period out of oestrus

weeks during the breeding season; others are more erratic. The frequency of heats in pedigree queens is also very variable. If a queen is mated but does not conceive, she will enter a state of pseudo-pregnancy (see below, left) before coming back into heat.

Spaying

This is a surgical procedure to neuter a queen. Under a general anaesthetic, the ovaries and entire uterus are removed through the abdomen. Despite the fact that spaying is a major operation, complications are rare and an uneventful recovery normally takes place within 10 days. The majority of queens not intended for breeding are spayed at the age of six months.

Advantages
• Spaying is immediate and 100 per cent effective.
• It removes problems of managing a queen in heat.

Disadvantages
• Spaying is a major procedure with inherent risks.
• It cannot be reversed.

BIRTH CONTROL USING DRUGS

Certain hormonal drugs can be used in the short term to suppress the signs of a heat, or to postpone an imminent heat. The drugs can also be administered at regular intervals to prevent heats in the long term. When they are stopped, the queen should eventually come back into heat. These drugs are only appropriate for queens who have had their first heat.

A healthcare plan for your kitten

If you are anything like me, you will never remember when you should be having your eyes tested, your teeth checked over by your dentist or your tetanus vaccination updated, but now you have your kitten's health to look after as well. Some healthcare tasks – such as feeding – obviously need to be carried out each day, and not even I would need reminding to do those. However, other very important procedures – such as vaccination and worming – must be undertaken at less frequent intervals, and so can be easier to overlook.

The following is a checklist that will help you to create a healthcare plan specifically customized to your kitten and to your lifestyle. Use the five-week diary extract opposite as a basis for creating a plan for your kitten's first 12 months of living with you. Provided that you do not omit any important procedures, this can be as basic or as detailed as you like.

Feeding

What to feed • Feed your kitten a diet based almost exclusively on one or more high-quality, prepared 'complete' foods that have been formulated and properly tested to meet the nutritional needs of growing kittens (see pages 58–60).

When to feed • Young kittens require frequent small meals because their digestive systems are easily overloaded. Given the opportunity, many older kittens and young adult cats also prefer to 'snack-feed': eating 10 meals a day is not unusual for a cat who is given free access to suitable food.

Changing to adult food • Gradually introduce one or more foods formulated and proven to meet the nutritional needs of adult cats when your kitten is fully grown at about 12 months old (see page 66).

Water • Ensure that fresh water is freely available to your kitten 24 hours a day (see pages 66–7).

TIMINGS OF TREATMENTS

Note that the exact timings of some procedures will vary, depending on the specific health problems to which your kitten may be exposed as a result of his environment and lifestyle. The timings of treatments will also depend on the products used, and on the prevailing views of the veterinary profession in your country. Ask at your vet centre for precise information relating to your own kitten.

Exercise

Every day, your kitten should be mentally stimulated as well as physically exerted – especially if he lives indoors or has only restricted outdoor access. Tailor your kitten's exercise regime to suit his abilities, lifestyle and interests. Options include the following.
• Indoor play with toys and a climbing frame or activity centre (see pages 83–5).
• Allowing your kitten the freedom to roam, climb, hunt and play outdoors.
• Lead walks on a harness (see page 87).

Grooming

At home • Give your kitten a quick groom daily, and a more thorough groom weekly (see pages 108–10).

With a professional groomer • If you have a long-haired kitten, he will benefit from a professional groom every six to 12 months.

Bathing • Only bath your kitten when it is absolutely necessary (see page 111).

Dental care

You should aim to brush your kitten's teeth and gums for about one minute once a day, using an appropriate toothbrush and toothpaste (see pages 112–13).

Home health-checks

Inputs • Monitor your kitten's food and water intake daily for any obvious changes.

Outputs • Monitor your kitten's urine and faeces daily for any obvious changes.

Behaviour • Monitor your kitten's behaviour all the time: sudden changes may be early signs of illness.

Anatomy • Carry out a full physical examination of your kitten once a week (see pages 106–7).

Weighing • Weigh your kitten once a week as part of his health-checks (see page 107). Always do this at the same time of day, and note down the results.

Veterinary health-checks

With a vet • Arrange for your kitten to be examined by your vet immediately after you collect him at eight weeks old (see pages 70–1), and subsequently at 12 weeks and 12 months old.

With a veterinary nurse • Your kitten should see his veterinary nurse regularly (ideally, every four weeks) for development checks and weighing.

Vaccinations

Note that any vaccination regime will depend on the prevalence of diseases in your area or country, as well as on the products used (see left). The following is an example of a typical regime.

Against feline calicivirus, feline herpesvirus 1 and feline leukaemia virus (see pages 119–20) • An injection at nine weeks, a second injection at 12 weeks and a 'booster' at 15 months.

Worming

Note that the precise regime for worming will depend on the predicted worm burden in your area or country, as well as on the products used (see opposite, below). The following timings should therefore be taken as general guides only.

Against tapeworms (see pages 114–15) • An initial dose at eight weeks; further doses every two to three months.

Against roundworms (see pages 115–16) • An initial dose at eight weeks, a second dose at 10 weeks, a third dose at 12 weeks; subsequent doses every three months.

Treatment of external parasites

Note that the precise regime will depend on the predicted parasite burden in your area or country, as well as on the products used (see opposite, below). The following is an example of a routine treatment against fleas (see also pages 116–17).

On a kitten • An initial treatment at 12 weeks; further treatments every two weeks.

In a house • Treatment should be carried out prior to a kitten's arrival, and then every four months.

Family planning

Male option • Surgical castration, or neutering, is normally carried out before a kitten is six months old (see page 122).

Female options • Regular hormonal treatment should begin after a kitten's first heat, or season, and be continued as appropriate; alternatively, surgical spaying, or neutering, is normally carried out when a kitten is about six months old, prior to her first heat (see page 123).

This extract from a healthcare plan covers the first five weeks after a kitten has been re-homed at the age of eight weeks; re-homing may be later for a pedigree kitten (see page 36). Use this example as a basis for developing a healthcare plan that is customized to your kitten's first 12 months with you.

Week 8

clean teeth (daily) .... ☑
quick groom (daily).. ☑
thorough groom .... ☑
health-check at home .... ☑
check weight ....date...............kg (lb)........
health-check with vet..........................date............
development check with veterinary nurse ....date............
first tapeworm dose ....date............
first roundworm dose...........................date............

Week 9

clean teeth (daily) .... ☑
quick groom (daily).. ☑
thorough groom... ☑
health-check at home .... ☑
check weight ....date...............kg (lb)........
first vaccination...................................date............

Week 10

clean teeth (daily) .... ☑
quick groom (daily).. ☑
thorough groom .... ☑
health-check at home .... ☑
check weight ....date...............kg (lb)........
second roundworm dose ....date............

Week 11

clean teeth (daily) .... ☑
quick groom (daily).. ☑
thorough groom .... ☑
health-check at home .... ☑
check weight ....date...............kg (lb)........

Week 12

clean teeth (daily) .... ☑
quick groom (daily).. ☑
thorough groom .... ☑
health-check at home .... ☑
check weight ....date...........kg (lb)........
health-check with vet..........................date............
development check with veterinary nurse ....date............
second vaccination..............................date............
third roundworm dose ....date............
flea treatment .... ☑

Index

ACKNOWLEDGEMENTS

The publishing of any book is a team effort, and I would like to express my sincere thanks to the many organizations and to the individuals – both human and feline – who have played a part in creating *The Complete Guide to Kitten Care*.

I am particularly grateful to the following friends and colleagues for their general advice and guidance, and for their specific contributions.
Dr John Bradshaw BA Phd Director of the Anthrozoology Institute of the University of Southampton (the only research centre in the UK dedicated to studying the behaviour of cats and dogs, and their relationship with man).
Erica Peachey BSc (Hons) Consultant in animal behaviour.
Dr Jo Wills BVetMed. MRCVS Veterinary surgeon and animal nutritionist.
John Down BVetMed. MRCVS Veterinary surgeon.
Elspeth Down BVetMed. MRCVS Veterinary surgeon.
John Robinson BDS (Lond.) Dentist to the veterinary profession.
Sue Parslow Editor of *Your Cat* magazine.
Peter Young Award-winning professional cat-groomer.
The publishing team Sam, Viv, Jane, Paul, Claire and Nina.

PUBLISHER'S ACKNOWLEDGEMENTS

Reed Illustrated Books would like to thank the following organizations and people for their help with photography, illustrations and modelling:
Mr A. Glue at Millbrooke Animal Centre (RSPCA), Chobham; Pet Plan Insurance; Peter Young at Posh Paws; Craig and Janet Irvine-Smith, Sue Holden, Liz McGauley and Anne Walton at Stonehenge Veterinary Hospital; Waltham Centre for Pet Care and Nutrition; Geoff Borin; Jane Burton and family; Mark Taylor; Hazel Taylor; Nick Goodall; Vicky Gray; Rosie Hyde; Jackie Chambers, and Louise and James; Vera Lopez; Alison, Mike and Grace Molan; Claire Musters; Nicola O'Connell; Mr and Mrs Paul and family; Nina Pickup; Sarah Pollock; Ina Weston; Tim Ridley; Herb Schmitz; Hunters Lodge Veterinary Surgery, Ewhurst.

PICTURE CREDITS

Animal Graphics Ltd/Angela Rixon 93.
Animal Photography/Sally Anne Thompson 89.
University of Bristol/Department of Companion Animals/Dr Frances Barr 17.
Jane Burton 38, 90, 121, 123 (top).
Dr Gary England/Royal Veterinary College 13 (below), 16 (top right and below right).
Oxford Scientific Films/Des and Jen Bartlett 8/London Scientific Films 114, 115, 116/John McCammon 118/Frank Schneidermeyer 80 (below).
Pet City 58.
Pedigree Pet Foods 59.
Reed International Books Ltd/Jane Burton 1, 2, 10, 12, 15, 16, 18, 19 (left and right), 20, 21, 22, 23 (left and right), 24, 25 (above and below), 26, 27 (above and below), 28, 29 (above and below), 30, 31 (above and below), 32 (above and below), 33 (above and below), 34 (above, below left and below right), 35 (above and below), 40, 41, 42, 43, 49, 52, 57 (above and below), 60 (above and below), 61, 62, 63 (above and below), 64, 65, 66, 67 (above and below), 68, 69, 70, 71, 72, 73, 74, 75, 76, 77 (left and right), 79 (below left and below right), 79 (above), 82, 83, 84, 85, 86, 98, 99 (above), 106 (left, centre and right), 107 (above, below left and below right), 108 (left, centre and right), 109, 110, 111 (above and below), 113, 117, 128/Nick Goodall 95, 97/Rosie Hyde 102 (above and below), 103, 104/Ray Moller 44, 45 top, 45 (below), 46, 47/Tim Ridley 3, 6, 54, 100, 101/Herb Schmitz 99 (below).
Jacket photography/Jane Burton (front, main picture and back)/Tim Ridley (front, author's photograph).
Illustrations/Adam Abel 51/Stefan Chabluk 9, 14 (below left and right), 36, 80, 101, 105, 123/Liz Gray 11, 13, 14 (top), 19, 56, 114, 115, 116, 122 (left and right)/Chris Orr 39, 87, 91.
John Robinson BDS (London) 112.
Tony Stone Images 36 (top), 37, 81/Jerome Tisne 48.
Your Cat **magazine**/Lesley Deaves (Jacket, back flap).
Zefa Picture Library Jacket (spine), 7, 9 (top), 55, 92.